I0449099

A COMMON SENSE PLATFORM
FOR THE 21ST CENTURY

Researched, written and formulated by B.K. Eakman
© October 2010

All rights reserved. No part of this book may be reproduced in any form or by any electronic or mechanical means, including information storage and retrieval systems, without permission in writing from the publisher, except by a reviewer who may quote brief passages in a review.

ISBN: 1452887721
EAN-13: 9781452887722

First Edition
October 2010

Midnight Whistler Publishers
http://www.midnightwhistler.com

A Common Sense Platform for the 21st Century is dedicated to **Pamela Gayle Harlan** (1953-2010) of Benson, Arizona, located near Tucson. Her insight and dedication to America's founding principles, her experience as a trusted civic leader, coupled to her zest for life and her election or appointment to many local and state offices enriched the lives of those around her and serves as the inspiration for this publication.

Here's What They're Saying:

Beverly Eakman's book is FANTASTIC! Not just the platform-type recommendations, but ALL of it. Every American needs to read it, preferably well before the national election in 2012.
--Joan Battey, writer-columnist, Apalachin, NY

I just read the following in Beverly Eakman's advance copy of her soon-to-be-released A Common-Sense Platform for the 21st Century. It will rock America. Seriously! "[Today's] children are supposed to become 'decision-makers' at the age of four, and child experts consider toddlers flushing their teddy bears down the toilet mature enough to weigh in global warming, re-cycling and 'civil unions'." Her new book has got, well, everything and I am so pleased to get to see an advance copy.

-- Roni Bell Sylvester, Publisher/owner, Land And Water USA; co-founder Good Neighbor Law (Denver, CO)

This shows how close we have come to being totally dominated and flummoxed by people bent on controlling us and our country. So many of us here [at NAS, Michigan] appreciate Bev Eakman's work.
-- Richard L. Cutler, Ph.D., former vice-president, Univ. of Mich. (retired), and past president, Nat'l Assoc. of Scholars, Michigan chapter

ROCK ON, BEV! Thank you so much for taking a simple concept and turning it into the coffin lid for progressive agenda.
--Dave Harlan, Tea Party, Benson, Arizona

In general, I am in agreement with at least 95% of what you wrote, or more. What you are attempting to do is not an easy task and still get most people's attention. It lays out the issues and it outlines some of the common-sense solutions, in detail. It is historical, informational and partly inspirational, all necessary elements to keep the reader's attention. I applaud you for what you have put into this excellent effort.
--Ron Ewart, president, National Association of Rural Landowners

TABLE OF CONTENTS

FOREWORD

In researching and penning this booklet, it was a shock to discover that none of the current Platforms, from the two most competitive political parties (Democrat and Republican) down to the least-well-known and even radical ones, would pass constitutional muster. Most of the Platforms strike one as "political-speak," a hodge-podge of random pet peeves garnered from the daily headlines, with little or no context. While headlines sell newspapers and get people to tune in to TV newscasts, they give no hint as to what important stories have been "spiked" (i.e., censored), or what information has been consigned to the cutting-room floor.

Additionally, no political party in recent decades had taken time to categorize, in a logical fashion, the fundamental issues facing Americans — not in the 20th century, nor in these opening years of the 21st. The section entitled "What Americans Want" seeks to remedy at least that situation for the time being.

Despite the bumbling history surrounding third parties in American politics, there has never been a better time to rethink the current two-party phenomenon that is tearing our nation apart. Some two-thirds of American citizens have no viable political party to represent them. Neither of the two major parties, Democrat nor Republican, serves the national interest. By the September 2010 primaries, their rhetoric was barely distinguishable from one another, even though Republicans technically had the advantage. No matter: Republican Ohio Rep. John A. Boehner suddenly switched positions to accommodate Democrats on dismantling Bush-era tax cuts during a recession, and actually helped his opponents equate people making $250,000 a year with billionaires. Such instant shifts of opinion are common in today's political climate and demonstrate a lack of firm principles.

The fact that Tea Party candidates who were thought to "have no chance" actually won in many of the September 2010 primary races confirms the perception that *all* existing parties, high-profile or not, are in dire need of a reality check. Columnist Jeffrey T. Kuhner hit the mark when he wrote that America "no longer has citizen legislators but rulers" and that our seat of government has become an "empire swollen with lobbyists, [career] bureaucrats, con artists and special interests."[1]

Unfortunately, those of us who know how Washington really works, also know the history and fate of third-party efforts. These are addressed in a later section of this booklet. The first order of business, however, is to detail exactly what issues — social, economic, national security, etc. — are in the forefront of citizen concern.

Thus, the first point: *Citizens'* concerns, as opposed to politicians' concerns. Despite today's seeming obsession with surveys and polls, career politicians and government bureaucrats view their self-serving notions

---

[1]   "Middle America Revolts," by Jeffrey T. Kuhner, *The Washington Times*, Oct. 22, 2010, p. B3.

as the only concerns worthy of merit. The populace per se is seen as convenient blocs of "nobodies" whose opinions count only in a muddled and abstract way.

The old saw that "statistics can be made to say anything" has proved disturbingly accurate, as publication of polls routinely mock the body politic with ambiguous findings. This is due, in part, to the way questions are posed. Respondents appear to be confused on nearly every issue, repeatedly contradicting themselves. The problem is exacerbated by the tiny samplings used to arrive at extremely large-scale statistical results.

In our Founders' day, candidates for public offices could, of course, more easily fool voters by tailoring their messages to their audiences. It was much harder for listeners to compare notes without the instant-communication tools we have today. Yet, they did better than us; and often were more sensitive to a "con" when they heard one. Perhaps they were not so distracted by the myriad diversions of modern life — hours spent commuting, chauffeuring children around, accom-modating hundreds of nuisance regulations and, finally, amusing themselves with tabloids and television.

Ironically, the Internet and nonstop newscasts like CNN have not generated any mass-motivation to compare and analyze campaign rhetoric or to reconcile voting records with pretty speeches. Modern communication has produced, instead, "information overload," which in turn has created an over-reliance on single-source outlets. These news sources each vie to be the "default" setting on everyone's personal computer and radio dial. The down side is that in an era when people can easily compare notes, they don't.

Those few who *do* keep tabs on what the other side is saying often discover something ominous at election time: The candidates listed on the sample ballot they receive with their polling-place information have declined to publicize anything about their stands on issues, their philosophy of government, or why they are running for office. In accessing several online services that publish comparative summaries at the county and district levels, one often finds a "no response" to requests for photographs, biographical and website information. A few candidates use Facebook and Twitter to get "friends" and "followers," but such pages read more like social-networking blurbs than any serious discussion of issues.

What one does find, oddly enough, are the same dozens of competing signs clumped together around transportation hubs and polling places, all with the names of candidates prominently displayed, but again, little concerning what any of them stand for. The only new strategy is the annoying diet of computerized phone calls ("robocalls") starting a week or so prior to election time, using either the candidate's or some famous somebody's, recorded voice asking the person who says "hello" to vote for so-and-so.

This campaign-election recipe has churned out a governing caste, more or less by default, whose "handlers" thoroughly understand the psychology of the electorate. Face time on television, like the proverbial newspaper photo-op, remains essential. But the substance of what is said is lost in an orgy of celebrity-like gamesmanship. They know only political junkies will bother to analyze what is said, and even that will be re-interpreted, edited and rewritten by a biased press. By election time, the public will be too exhausted or confused to significantly alter the legislative landscape.

Just as non-assimilating illegal immigrants are viewed as easy voting fodder (which partially explains why officials wink at illegal immigration and voter fraud), the rest of the public tends to be viewed as merely fickle, not alienated or disgruntled. In other words, professional handlers and campaign managers tend to see elections in terms of advertising and public relations, not as a real referendum on the positions of the candidates — regardless of assertions to the contrary. The result is low voter turnouts, especially in local and state primary elections, which is how the characters who wind up on the national stage jump-start their résumés.

Moreover, the impression of active political participation in America is more fiction than fact. Nearly everyone has an *opinion*, yes, but individual involvement and input continues to decline. The very existence of ever-more-passionate calls to "get-out-the-vote" could well be taken as a barometer of political disaffection, and much of the cause can be laid at the feet of the major political parties which have dominated the scene and issued the marching orders for over a century.

Into this morass comes new touch-screens and computerized voting, which are subtly changing the dynamics of the electoral process. While large-scale intrusions into the secret ballot have not yet occurred, any savvy information-technology specialist could explain several ways of cross-matching or tagging a voter's name with his or her voting-machine key card to reveal either *how* a particular individual voted or simply compromise entire stacks of anonymous ballots. The speed with which "spammers" and hackers have been able to access sensitive computer systems, personal and otherwise, should serve as a warning.

Add to that, sophisticated marketing capabilities that can turn charismatic, but ethically challenged, unknowns into "stars" and "starlets" virtually overnight, while denying a forum to respectable candidates who have meticulously and successfully raised support for their positions, and you have ballots headed for the compost.

Technology never *un*-invents itself. Thus, all these factors must be addressed if the uniquely American experiment called a self-governing Republic is to be maintained through the remainder of this century, much less beyond. It is to this cause that a rational, Common Sense platform is dedicated.

Introduction
THE PRESENT STATE OF THE UNION
(a.k.a. "the REPUBLIC")

When Thomas Paine wrote *Common Sense* and *Age of Reason*, he did so as a maverick, back when independent deliberations (or, "thinking outside the box") carried no stigma. The early success of *Common Sense* was a complete surprise to Mr. Paine and lifted him from obscurity to fame. Paine was also self-educated — something that was common even in the time of Abraham Lincoln, but which is also frowned upon today. Paine was not the most religious among his colleagues, or even the most learned. But his belief that thoughts ought to be allowed to "mature over time" is a stand-out, especially today when every toddler flushing his or her teddy bear down the toilet is deemed a "decision-maker" by child experts, and when views expressed at age 16, without the benefit of factual knowledge or experience, are considered sufficiently legitimate to allow these opinionated youth to weigh in on topics ranging from "global climate disruption," to stem-cell research to "civil unions."

In point of fact, Paine's own thoughts had evolved by the time he had written a subsequent tome, *The Rights of Man*, which established him as one of the foremost thinkers of his era. One can agree or disagree with his logic; that is not the issue. The point is that in a free society a person should have the luxury of changing opinions; the individual ought not to be chained to former, and perhaps less mature, viewpoint. That is the essence of "free conscience," without which liberty cannot exist. For this reason, Thomas Paine remains a "great" among American thinkers.

One of the most ominous harbingers of our time has become the student questionnaire or survey, not so much because a pupil is asked to express an opinion (ideally, schoolchildren should be writing lots of paragraphs supporting and opposing a variety of positions), but because whatever one says at a young age is recorded for posterity in a databank. Later, the child's multiple-choice viewpoint is trotted out, to potential embarrassment, should he or she aspire to a political appointment as head of a government agency, or to candidacy for some public office, or to a management role in a large firm. Most 16-year-olds are naïve enough to imagine that an opinion uttered in the innocence of youth is "confidential" in the sense of being anonymous, or at least private. But such is not the case. There is no way to prove a data-file has been purged or that there is no backup copy.

The American ideal of free thought has vanished in a hodge-podge of comity, consensus, teamwork and affability. Independent thought is laden with pejoratives: "dogmatic," "intolerant," "inflexible" — or the ultimate conversation-stopper: "mentally instable," as per a September 2010 Comment by Pennsylvania Democratic Governor Edward G. Rendell that the Republican Party was "slowly but surely being taken over by wackos." While "thinking outside the box" still carries a connotation of virtue, actually daring to do so publicly is equated with wackiness, no matter who does it.

Just as Benjamin Franklin feared in 1787, it took only some 200 years for politicians of the prevailing political parties to view the issues they debated, no matter how mundane (e.g., childrearing or food choices), as hopelessly complicated for all but themselves and a cottage industry of counterfeit "experts." Opposing views from the masses, even highly credible persons with advanced degrees, increasingly were dismissed if they deviated from whatever was trendy.

Since the early 1950s, nearly all criticisms of government and policy have been cast in collective terms, giving short shrift to individual input and personal responsibility. One must be "politically connected," or stand in danger of being brushed off and marginalized. Thus, the proliferation of computer "blogs," readers' Comment boxes appended to online news sites, and letters-to-the-editor. Most of these forums are considered "prattle" by pundits, policymakers and journalists, who decline to read them or respond. This has resulted in groups of citizen-journalists launching their own web sites, in order to bring legitimacy and urgency to their observations on the news. An example is Pajamas Media, a name derived from a dismissive comment made by former news executive vice-president, Jonathan Klein, of CBS during the Killian documents affair, when then-CBS anchorman Dan Rather failed during the run-up to the 2004 election to authenticate a memo demeaning President George W.

Bush's old military service record in the Coast Guard: "You couldn't have a starker contrast between the multiple layers of checks and balances at [the TV-news show] *60 Minutes* and a guy sitting in his living room in his pajamas," Klein quipped.

Dan Rather essentially lost his job and status over what was perceived as a deliberate, politically motivated inaccuracy, and Pajamas Media, through a succession of name changes, began attracting many established Commentators, political analysts, radio and television producers and professional pollsters. But, like so many upstart media outlets, its original mission of catching discrepancies and challenging conventional wisdom became diluted and directionless, especially when, for lack of political savvy, the fledgling organization excluded candidates like Ron Paul because he had failed to make the one-percent cut in a 2008 Gallup straw-poll for the U.S. Presidential race, and instead aired interviews with individuals who weren't even running, such as Al Sharpton and Al Gore.

To the degree that marginalization and belittling of the politically "unconnected" individual have morphed into art forms, the United States no longer can expect leadership, bold and imaginative action or principled government. Creativity and originality are the stuff of an Amusement Culture — a world of electronic gadgets, fantasy-football games, and "shock-jock" entertainers, all pushing an already overstuffed envelope in search of the almighty dollar.

Unsurprisingly, innovative and ground-breaking approaches to tough ethical, social, legal, medical and technological problems are no longer pursued in a way that encourages ingenuity and resourcefulness, because those are qualities of *individuals*, not of collectives. Americans have been conditioned for nearly half a century to value the group, or team, more than "idiosyncratic" individuality.

For all these reasons, the United States has ceased to be the citadel of political thought and autonomy that other nations once wished to emulate. Instead, our Nation is devolving into just one more overbearing, top-heavy bureaucracy that controls through intimidation, red tape, paperwork and redistribution under some convenient pretext.

Soon enough, such a government doesn't even require a pretext. A Marxist-like takeover of Congress in 2008, has launched audacity and intimidation to new heights in a hurried effort to finish off any remaining principles of Jeffersonian-style democracy, such as individual conscience and property rights.

A word is in order here about property rights: Some claim that the U.S. Constitution says nothing about property rights. That is partly true, but requires some context. Patrick Henry refused to endorse the new constitution specifically *because* it said nothing about protecting individual property rights. His opposition forced James Madison to create the Bill of Rights and the Fifth Amendment. In addition, there exist dozens of Commentaries by the likes of Founders George Washington, John Adams and Thomas Jefferson in their deliberations back and forth concerning the absolute necessity of property rights in order that true freedom might exist. The Federalist papers show clearly their thinking on this issue, and they fully believed that the Constitution, including the Fifth Amendment, served to protect property rights. It is unfortunate that the today's educators no longer see fit, in most cases, to expose K-12 students to the contents of the Federalist Papers so that they can see for themselves the various arguments, rationales and justifications behind the U.S. Constitution. That is how mistaken perceptions on the Constitution proliferate.

Republicans leaders are as culpable as Democrats, as they have for years gone along to get along and caved to political correctness, apologizing again and again for perceived slights and failing to dig in their heels when the situation calls for it. Insistence on including the Federalist Papers in any U.S. history curriculum as a "compelling state interest" would have been one of those kinds of issues. Instead, they have surrendered to lobbyists for drug-and-sex educators, who appropriated the term "compelling state interest" for their own ends, and helped to expand the U.S. Department of Education into the wasteful behemoth that is has become.

Expansion of government agencies has resulted in the creation of so many regulations and criminal laws over the past 40 years that they have become "traps for…law-abiding citizens," according to former Attorney General Edwin Meese III. Whereas the Constitution identified just three federal crimes — piracy, treason and counterfeiting — and the first Congress stipulated only 17 in the Crimes Act of 1790, the "best estimate is that the federal code now delineates more than 4,500 [crimes], with [f]ederal regulations creat[ing] tens of thousands more," Meese wrote in a September 16, 2010, column for *The Washington Times*.[2] This has resulted in the "over-criminalizing" of Americans — or "*uber-criminalization*," also referred to by some as "gotcha justice." As Meese puts it, these laws "involve conduct that is not inherently wrong but [which] has been made criminal only because an...unelected bureaucracy...has decreed it so."

The same Boomer generation that once demonstrated against limitations and rules, now can't seem to get enough of them. Had Boomers spent more time on their studies than demonstrating, they would know that this is a signature move of all totalitarian wannabes to usurp control.

Thus, the two terms, "ruling elite" and "ruling class," are flourishing among the opinion pages and over the airwaves. But these are not quite apt descriptors of today's current governing body in America. Both expressions imply some economic, ethnic or cultural relationship. What we have is more like a caste system, which is even more rigid, especially in terms of patronage, preferential treatment and political power. Caste rewards its stewards according to family lineage and interconnected power bases, always demanding deference and acquiescence. Accordingly, grants are dispensed and contracts are awarded to groups and individuals whose loyalty can be counted on to turn a blind eye when the governing caste bends rules, passes

---

[2]   According to the Congressional Research Service, the number of criminal offenses is officially uncountable, but CRS estimates go as high as 300,000.

Executive Orders, adds cabinet posts, pads the judiciary, and appoints various "czars" to fulfill what has become government's primary objective (regardless of political party) — bypassing the people and imposing an agenda that runs counter to their wishes.

Thomas Paine understood, as did contemporaries like Thomas Jefferson, Benjamin Franklin and John Adams, that the factionalism resulting from this sort of governance would irreparably damage the fledgling nation, just as surely as armies from without. So, while a party system has always existed in one form or another, the Framers of our Constitution recognized that Americans, at some point, needed to speak with one voice.

That meant, of course, a degree of assimilation, which in turn required that education, whether from governesses or schoolhouses, must expose youngsters to a common store of heroes and villains, ideals and virtues, language and culture. In other words, it was logical that a base, or foundation, be inculcated *before* young pupils went about expressing their opinions.

The notion of a common store of basic knowledge, unfortunately, has been swept away in modern times. *Diversity* is in reality "particularism"; *multiculturalism* is intended to divide, not unite. What little knowledge *is* inculcated tends to be dictated by the fleeting winds of political correctness. The child's authority figures revolve around pals and classmates — not adults and parents. In fact, childrearing is considered best left to "unbiased experts," while a parent's role is to amass sufficient income to pay for the continued lifestyles of the ruling caste and its various agendas.

All this has culminated in vast changes for American society. Children remain immature longer, despite any physical appearance to the contrary. American adults tend to be less educated than their forebears, regardless of how many college degrees they have. High school graduates often cannot write a reasoned, articulate paragraph.

Into this morass is wedged a predominantly two-party system, neither of which today serves its constituents well. Government at every level has spiraled out of control with virtually no accountability to the electorate. Disregard for our Constitution and founding documents permeates every facet of American life, the core ideals of the Nation having been all but banned and obliterated. Those who heed the message to "get involved" and seek to revive the Nation's constitutional heritage become disenchanted for a number of reasons — among them, marginalization by a media that is supposed to be open and unbiased; the struggle for the minds of children by educators, advertisers and entertainers; nonstop, mostly manufactured, crises that continually vie for public attention; a crumbling infrastructure that causes time-consuming inconveniences; and a national security/crime-fighting force that increasingly targets upstanding citizens for trivial infractions instead of focusing ferocious crimes that cost taxpayers a fortune and even end their lives.

Hampering efforts at reform has been the ongoing battle for funding by competing special interests more interested in preserving their "turf" than in coordinating a strategy to battle specific abuses and usurpations by government and its proxies. This turns off the electorate and fosters non-participation. Most of the few organizations that still speak out against the ruling caste and its agendas too often conduct themselves like exclusive fraternities and sororities, minus the secret handshake. Their leaders are typically "unavailable" and unresponsive to constituents. Staffers are paid to turn away even well-educated citizens, lumping them all together as necessary nuisances. Instead, elected officials attempt to console this backbone of society with scripted responses by phone and letter, so that their offices can get back to the business of fabricating direct-mail surveys (which will go unheeded), instituting self-serving polls, and launching $400-a-plate extravaganzas that they believe will bring in the grand amounts of money required to do whatever job they pretend they are doing.

Thus, unless a constituent is "connected" to someone "important" in Washington or Hollywood, he or she is shooed away. Such tactics, while enhancing the perceived power of the governing caste, actuality diminish it, because citizens of talent and ideas who might otherwise be helpful soon give up and flee to the comfort of their television sets, from which they sit and seethe. Eventually, the seeds of revolution are planted, "government" at all levels becomes the "enemy," and public support is lost — usually permanently.

Today in the United States, more than two political parties exist, but none besides Democrats and

Republicans has yet made a significant electoral showing. This may be changing, as the rank-and-file becomes increasingly dissatisfied, sometimes without being able to articulate the exact cause of their angst but nevertheless unsupportive of the status quo. As America goes the way of Europe, and edges toward a welfare state, the Nation is divided as never before, demonstrating an irrationality born of frustration and apathy: the perfect recipe for a future police state.

Aware of increasing antipathy from the masses, the governing caste circulates memos to federal and state employees, urging them to report anything resembling violent militias or "lone wolves" with a grudge. With each passing administration, the governing caste flexes more muscle, "throws its weight around" just to prove it can, and then gauges the public mood to ascertain how much more it can get away with.

Today's climate of over-regulation, bailouts, frivolous rules and regulations would have infuriated the World War I and II generations which fought and died to prevent such an occurrence. Sadly, the now-adult graduates of America's K-12 post-war schools and universities, especially those born between the years 1957 (the launch of Sputnik) and the 1980s, cannot grasp the speed with which these sea-changes in American life have occurred. Like good little conformists, they view the governing caste as their "betters." *They need their peers more than they need their principles.* They live in a world cut off from earlier generations of adults — a world of splintered families and impersonalized day-care, an existence of electronic gadgets, tacky clothes, prurient entertainment, epidemic sexually transmitted diseases and culture rot that serves to inflame the spirit instead of to inspire and calm.

Moreover, the present system of political patronage has outlived its usefulness. It has proved incapable of pursuing a rational, Common Sense set of goals, standards or expectations. It is time to construct a definitive political platform that cuts through party affiliation (without the moniker of phony "bipartisanship") — a platform that invokes the ideals of the Nation's Founders, yet which accommodates the needs of a 21st Century, sovereign America.

Section 1.- OUTSIDE THE "COMFORT ZONE": Changes We Can't Believe In

> "It is a mistake, in my view, to assume that all people want to be free, in the sense of the American pioneers. I think they much prefer to be comfortable; as the establishment of welfare states almost everywhere ... has shown. [T]he greatest of all freedoms, the one that more people want more than any other, is the freedom from responsibility and consequences." – Theodore Dalrymple, "Do we all want freedom?" *Axess Magazine*, Oct. 17, 2010

British writer Theodore Dalrymple (a.k.a. Anthony Daniels), a physician and former prison doctor, recently observed that people do not necessarily want to be free; they want to be *comfortable*. As if to confirm his suspicions, in the United States every election cycle shows an increased number of citizens dependent on the government for their basic needs, until we are fast approaching Europe's status as an Entitlement State. Take a September 2010 Gallup survey showing Americans relying on government health-care programs *over* employer-provided health-insurance options. "Broadly speaking, government health coverage has been steadily rising since the start of the recession, while employer-based insurance has been declining.

Concomitantly, the number of uninsured Americans has gone up," stated Gallup's website.[3]

And that's just one element in a whole laundry list of fundamental necessities.

Such thinking creates a vicious cycle: new programs of federal and state spending, followed by increased public debt from which eventually there is no escape. This stands in stark contrast to the logic and values endorsed by the Founders of our Nation in the Declaration of Independence, the Constitution and Bill of Rights: self-sufficiency, self-reliance, self-discipline and self-determination — ideals that form the cornerstones of self-government.

In order to be *completely* comfortable, there are those who expect others to behave as they would, or at least as they *proclaim* they would. That means rules, and lots of them. On that basis, the populace gets an increasingly regimented and regulated State, with all the accompanying apparatus of a bureaucracy tasked with oversight, on-site inspections and enforcement. Bureaucracies grow because there is powerful incentive to "find things" and enforce regulations.

That is also how government "creates jobs."

Most of the people inadvertently supporting "progressive" policies and "equitable" legislation have no idea what is coming down the pike until it hits them, personally, in a way they never expected. That's when the term "no free lunch" hits home, when the powers entrusted to government to force others to do something

---

[3]   Gallup website: http://www.gallup.com/poll/143006/gov-healthcare-recession-began.aspx.

supposedly noble and wise are suddenly used *against* the very persons who, in effect, voted to regulate *other people*.

Health care is a recent example everyone can relate to, as it increasingly dominates the news. Universal health insurance sounds noble. That government should bear the lion's share of responsibility for underwriting everybody's health coverage strikes many as "fair" — meaning equitable. Deep down, of course, even the most committed collectivist knows that the extremely wealthy — multimillionaires and above — will neither avail themselves of, nor expose their families to, government-underwritten "equitable" care. They will pay for, and receive, what is known as "concierge medicine," in which one pays a large annual fee up front to a physician — some $20,000 or more — for the privilege of 24/7 access by phone, e-mail or face-to-face contact. That is, the doctor will make house calls at any hour, will meet the patient at the emergency room to coordinate any tests or treatments, will refer the patients to the best specialists should any be required, and will assure that the patient is not denied medication for pain and suffering. That means, no waiting on a gurney in the emergency room hallway, no arguments over whether this or that medication is "covered" or "allowed," enjoying privacy and dignity while procedures are in progress and keeping loved ones informed and nearby if the patient so desires. In other words, it means medicine as it used to be practiced for nearly everyone — before the days of either private or public insurance coverage. The only ones waiting in the hall in full view of spectators then either lived in backwoods communities, were known criminals, deadbeats, or malingerers. So while medical technology per se has never been better, all but the exceedingly rich are treated as deadbeats and malingerers today.

Medicare and Medicaid should have served as a warning as to what would happen once impersonal insurance carriers and government bureaucrats began determining health-care benefits. But because so many people carried supplemental plans of some sort, and prices continued to rise precipitously, they swallowed the pinch at tax time, paid the exorbitant premiums, filled out the often-futile paperwork and accepted declining personal attention as the fate of non-millionaires.

Then, in 2010 something happened that shook many people awake. Big Brother not only suggested that everyone should eat more fruits and vegetables, and ordered schools to eject burgers and fries in favor of "more healthful alternatives," but government began hinting that the mandate to purchase health insurance just might be predicated upon eating the "right" foods.

For the present, the issue is whether to tax sugar-sweetened drinks, including juices and sports beverages, like "sin" taxes on cigarettes. But groups like Americans Against Food Taxes are justifiably reading a bit more into it. What about ice cream, after all? In a nationwide AAFT ad, mothers are featured inside grocery stores with their shopping carts saying: "I can decide what to buy without government help. The government is just getting too involved in our personal lives."

It doesn't take a rocket scientist to see that "universal" health insurance will not be sustainable. Medicare, Medicaid and Social Security, after all, are already moving into the red. One way to cut people off the insurance rolls would be to revoke it if they purchase the "wrong" foods. In the age of computerized surveillance, where government agencies can find out anything, any time and access any record, it is hardly far-fetched to imagine an examination of grocery receipts. A computerized list is printed out and handed to you as you leave the store. Your discount card ("club" card or whatever a grocery store pleases to call it) has a bar code linked to your name, address and phone number. All of this, of course, ensures that you can return purchases you find unsatisfactory and get a discount on the specials of the week at your local market. But it can, and will (eventually) also be data-shared with important "others" who either want to sell you something or have different sort of "stake" in your affairs, including your supposed "well-being."

Speed limits established by government were also deemed noble undertakings, as were mandatory vehicle insurance, observance of red lights and stop signs, laws against reckless driving (i.e., tailgating on freeways, being distracted by trivialities, frequent lane changes to save a few seconds), and eliminating dirty vehicle emissions.

But what happened? Speed *limits* soon morphed into speed *traps*. Speed traps started out as sudden and ridiculously low limits aimed at enhancing local revenue, usually placed strategically at the bottom of a hill or around a curve where police cars could hide. At first, these traps were only occasional nuisances that required local law enforcement officers to waste time more appropriately spent curbing burglary and violent crime for an hour or so of radar or laser duty.

But it got worse. Speed bumps began emerging nearly everywhere (at some $1,200-$2,000 apiece) in the 1990s. These expensive irritations are paid for by taxpayers and constitute outright hindrances to ambulances, drivers with disabilities and vehicles facing icy or snowy conditions. Then came even more expensive cameras, along with arbitrary fines that actually *caused* accidents. Traffic lights were deliberately altered to shorten the timeframes on yellow-amber lights so that city and county governments could *generate* even more revenue while disregarding public safety. As for mandatory auto insurance, every fine assessed by various traffic cameras increases drivers' annual premiums, meaning that people either pay fines, or take off work to fight nuisance tickets. Records show that since the installation of cameras, the relative percentage of tickets successfully contested has gone up.

But bureaucrats know that taking off work every month or so to fight a ticket is not cost-effective in the long run, so they continue bilking the public. Also, contractors who install the cameras have been known to get kickbacks from the increased revenue.

Whatever happened to reckless driving? To all the law enforcement officers who were going to stop tailgaters, drivers weaving in and out of traffic, turn-signal violations, and kids drag-racing and doing "wheelies" on city streets? Well, police departments claim they don't have the manpower to perform these functions. How about those "aggressive-driver" imaging cameras? Are they being used to target reckless drivers and to save the lives of motorists, or are they being utilized to comb certain time-frames for vehicles suspected of offenses completely unrelated to driving or even terrorism?

And what of annual vehicle-emissions inspections, which started as a five-year project that would then be phased out? Every driver knows the answer to that.

These kinds of questions, of course, describe the proverbial slippery slope. More troubling, though, is that modern Americans, on the whole, do not equate accelerating incursions into their daily lives or the overabundance of rules, regulations and handouts with control, dependency and collectivism. Indeed, talk of self-sufficiency today is akin to being a called a "loner," and we are reminded daily that loners are dangerous, on a level with sociopaths.

Similarly, the public does not connect successive financial crises with political instability — even though chains of economic disasters almost always end with a highly regulated super-state in which self-determinism for the masses is not tolerated.

Thus, the problems we face today are not so much about Democrats versus Republicans, Liberals versus Conservatives, or left-wingers versus right-wingers. None of these terms, in fact, mean what they did originally. What the Nation's problems boil down to is self-determination versus regimentation. Regardless of political party, most candidates — or at least their handlers — understand the American psyche all too well: *People would rather be comfortable than self-reliant; popular, not self-sufficient.*

Thanks to nearly 40 years of watered-down schooling, most of today's adults do not recall (or just haven't been alive long enough to know) exactly how we got where we are now. Consequently, many of us have become closet Marxist-socialists without even realizing it, actually believing the adage "from each according to his ability, to each according to his need," even when we insist otherwise. Since the eras of Woodrow Wilson and Franklin D. Roosevelt, we have been subtly lured into accepting Nanny-style notions like Social Security, Medicare, "free" public education, food stamps, government-supplied workers' compensation and a host of other programs that, once mandated through taxes, tend to take on a life of their own. Every time we accede to such ideas as "leveling the playing field," "the graduated income tax" and "programs for the less fortunate," we unwittingly buy in to Karl Marx's socialist adage.

It is popular to say that the U.S. "won" the Cold War, but the truth is that the same Marxist-based socialism that turned communistic when practiced by the Soviet Union and its satellite regimes did a tremendous amount of damage before the inevitable collapse. Only East Germany is bouncing back, with a whole lot of help from West Germany, which is certainly not free in the sense Americans think of that term. Sadly, many True Believers of the Marxist-socialist mold are still among us, swaying even those who would deny any such leanings vehemently. While these True Believers may no longer be the totalitarians shown in old war footage, in the sense of hosing their opposition down with machine guns, they nevertheless cut their teeth on the kind of community activism that would have won accolades from both Hitler and Stalin; that is to say, they have well-paying jobs manipulating the masses — careers at which the old masters of the 1930s and 40s excelled and passed along. They see free markets as ravenous, self-sufficiency as unrealistic and self-determination as reckless.

In 1960, the historian Henry Wriston complained in a *Wall Street Journal* article that the individual was no longer "at the core of our political, religious and economic thought." Individualism, not comfort, he said, was the price of freedom. Today, however, the obsession with comfort extends even to meetings in which individuals are supposed to be debating things, thrashing out problems, offering opposing solutions and alternatives. Instead, we are driven by consensus-thinking; if we cannot be civil, at least we will be comfortable. But as Mr. Wriston noted, "nothing in the Bill of Rights promises that the freedoms there guaranteed can be enjoyed in a serene atmosphere." Speaking out on controversial matters, he insisted, requires *dis*comfort if freedom is to amount to anything.

Parents of the Boomer generation were the ones reading those words then. But even though they had recently fought a horrific World War and held high ideals and standards, they wanted their own children to have something they didn't: comfort.

Younger Americans tend to believe that *because* Germany surrendered in 1945, and *because* the old Soviet Union fell in 1989, it means that Nazism, communism, socialism and Marxism all are dead. Yet, America is surrounded (in Latin America and elsewhere) with Marxist-copycat regimes, whether their populations earnestly toe the collectivist line or not. Tyrannies running rampant in the Middle East and Africa are possibly more repressive than Hitler's Third Reich, minus the sophistication and systematization. Even the Taliban and Al Qaeda, living in caves along the Afghan-Pakistani border, learned a thing or two about effective public relations campaigns, manipulating the press and twisting laws to suit their needs. Where did they learn these things? From their former Soviet occupiers.

None of this seems to occur to large swathes of Americana, or to its leaders at the state and national levels. Why? Because *a higher premium is assigned to being comfortable than to being free*. Indeed, Americans have come to *equate* being comfortable **with** being free.

Like the garbage disposal in the kitchen, and the toilet in the bathroom, nobody in possession of these conveniences is in any hurry to trudge outside with sack-loads of smelly garbage every night or to pay a visit to the outhouse at five o'clock in the morning. This is entirely understandable. Westerners deem themselves "beyond" such indignities.

The same mindset, unfortunately, applies to "entitlement" programs, especially once everyone has paid into them. Nobody is enthusiastic about giving them up, even when they are actually counterproductive. The general feeling is: I was forced to pay for it, now I want my share back, with interest. On top of that, Americans have been conditioned to be "fair," but fairness increasingly translates into provide others with everything that we ourselves are struggling to afford: "from each according to his ability, to each according to his [or her] need."

Concentration of power must be fought wherever it exists or the individual simply will not count. That means the more highly centralized the government, the greater and harsher its reach into the states and local communities, and finally into every nook and cranny of private enterprise and activity. A ten-year-old is slapped with a fine in New York for setting up a lemonade stand without a license. A young teen is not only arrested, but handcuffed, simply for eating one French-fry on in a Washington, D.C., subway.

Certainly big societies like ours require strong leadership, but the power must be spread, with *ultimate control in the hands of average, (hopefully literate) people, a majority of whom place a premium on morality and decency.*

It is not as though Americans have had *no* inkling of the shocking events now almost daily in the news. Yet, suddenly we are startled and overwhelmed by the blatant and coordinated nature of measures which government at all levels has indulged, in violation of what little we remember of our Constitutional ideals. Taken together, certain ominous actions have recently frightened us to action; among them:

- A transparent agenda to so deplete government funds through various "obligations" as to bring our nation to a financial standstill, thereby providing all the excuse a federal entity would require to nationalize key industries and businesses and other sectors.

- Increasing assaults by the federal agencies upon America's constitutional order, including (but not limited to) attacks upon all state and local efforts to control illegal immigration, "uber-criminalization" of law-abiding citizens through thousands of petty federal regulations (the Founders recognized only three federal crimes), and an attempt to nationalize health care via mandatory insurance.

- A system of interconnected data collection instruments, begun in schools and the military in the late 1970s, which have now morphed into surveillance tools aimed not only at schoolchildren or the defense of our nation, but at adult activities as benign as their online book purchases. Such shenanigans are ostensibly intended to deter violence and conduct surveys, but in reality creating a means of estimating anticipated levels of resistance to programs, policies and procedures, increasing the potential for political persecution.

- Undeclared wars ("military actions") aimed at appeasing our enemies (via costly reconstruction and humanitarian projects) without the requisite demand for total surrender of armaments and cessation of hostilities, instead of using our military solely in the defense of our people and America's national interests.

- Soak-the-(so-called)-rich schemes that generate class warfare and have filtered down to include mega-taxes on "rich," upper-middle-class incomes of $250,000, which in most major cities is not enough to send two children to private school during the K-12 years.

- Federal subsidies to radical, anti-American groups like ACORN (Association of Community Organizations for Reform Now)[4], coupled to loopholes in the tax code for 501c4 "advocacy groups," and to jihadist activist factions (e.g., The Muslim Brotherhood) that allow them to operate nationwide under false pretenses, promoting their fanatical agendas, including paying interlopers to protest and incite riots.

- Aggressive interference in the education of our young, an action which includes pressure to drug and provide "social services" to children instead of teaching them. (Parents are so alienated in the State of Delaware that education officials considered *paying* them to become involved in their children's schooling).

- Approval for a dubious "cultural center" (Cordoba House, a name signifying the 784 AD conquest in Spain, the purpose of which was to destroy any competing houses of worship and impose Shariah law), coupled with an accompanying mosque. In

---

[4]   ACORN frequent partners with government in specific projects.

the present climate (since the September 11, 2001, attacks) both proposals serve to honor and appease foreign combatants at the site of the Ground Zero attacks in New York, inasmuch as there exist of some 100 similar centers and 1,200 mosques, more than enough to accommodate the small fraction of Moslems among our populace, already inside the country.

- A federal agency (the U.S. State Department) applies *U.S. tax dollars* to building and renovating mosques in some 27 countries since the 9/11 attacks by "religious" extremists,[5] at the same time that Christian icons are being systematically ejected from public places, even when privately funded, based on a deliberate misreading of the Establishment Clause (e.g., the August 18, 2010, decision to remove a 12-foot cross erected in 1968 by the privately funded Utah Highway Patrol Association to honor a deceased trooper in Utah).

- A call by the Speaker of the House to *investigate resisters* to the aforementioned mosque at Ground Zero, opening the door to investigations targeting "resisters" to any other policy, program or project promoted by the ruling caste.

- Creation of a forum for the mastermind of the worst attack ever on American soil (in reality, a pre-emptive strike mischaracterized as rogue "terrorism"), giving a foreign militant, Khalid Shaihk Mohammed, legal and constitutional

---

[5] See reports from the Canada Free Press and National Center for Policy Analysis, among others.

protections previously reserved for U.S. citizens.

The list above comprises a mere sampling of the most recent abuses of the public trust. A more complete cataloging of actual usurpations follows in Section 4.

Since World War II, our war-weary populace has been lulled into a false sense of security. This has stemmed from two factors: First of all, we won the wars. While it is true that we lost many thousands of soldiers, our country per se came through the ordeal relatively unscathed. Save Pearl Harbor in Hawaii (not then a State), no buildings were toppled; nobody was stepping over dead bodies in the street — unlike out allies in Europe. Secondly, since everyone seemed to be immigrating **to** the United States, rather than **escaping** from it, we concluded that our constitutional freedoms were safe from significant tampering. But Norman Thomas, the six-time Socialist Party candidate for U.S. President, knew better. He prophesied in a 1944 speech:

> **"The American people will never *knowingly* adopt socialism. But, under the name of 'liberalism,' they will adopt every fragment of the socialist program, until one day America will be a socialist nation, without knowing how it happened...."**

Thus did entitlement programs become entrenched; they could not be dislodged or de-institutionalized. Unlike personal computers and high-definition televisions — both voluntary purchases — government entitlements could be alternately exploited and destabilized, just to keep the electorate in a constant state of anxiety and panic.

Today, the collective spirit of entitlement trumps our constitutional freedoms, overturning 200 years of support for the bracing venture of risk and reward. This decidedly un-American, socialistic mind-set has its roots in the nihilistic philosophies launched by the New Progressives and Mental Hygiene Movement advocates before and immediately following World War II. These eventually morphed into "The Self-Actualizing Society" — a psychology-based term that replaced self-determination as an ideal and turned the self-sacrificing ethic of the War years into the "Me Generation" of the Boomer years.

It happened like this: In 1946, Dr. Brock Chisholm, representing the World Federation of Mental Health, argued in favor of "freedom *from* morality" (as had Erich Fromm in Germany), urging an "eventual eradication of right and wrong." The traditional upbringing of children, he insisted, was making everyone "mentally ill." He advised that "the race ... be freed of its crippling burden of good and evil."

This dictum constituted the opening salvo in an undeclared war against the ideals supporting constitutional government. It goes far beyond religious admonitions against "sparing the rod." Morality is a hallmark any civilized society and, therefore, to a large extent, it is non-negotiable. But nihilists and closet Marxists tended to view morality as a religious, essentially Judeo-Christian, construct, which suited their purposes at the time. The public at large was blindsided by the twisted logic of Dr. Chisholm and his colleagues, and in the end capitulated to what they saw as an attractive package called "self-actualization" (a term coined by Abraham Maslow).

The notions articulated by Dr. Chisholm and the new breed of "progressives" were repeated and well-publicized until they became staples of a burgeoning industry portraying itself as "mental hygiene." Soon, child psychology, the "free-to-be" anarchist movement (aimed at young adults) and even feminism picked up the kernel concept: **Guilt Causes Neurosis**. This idea chipped away at parental control, childrearing, art, entertainment and school discipline and produced a sea-change that became embedded in the entire culture — politics included.

By the late 1950s, the way had been cleared for moral and ethical degeneracy, which spilled over into government and served to activate the "entitlement mentality" among Baby Boomer and post-Boomers. We were on the way to distorting the timeless principles that the Framers of the Constitution had so carefully invoked. Many *faux* social movements followed: "*faux*" because the justifications underlying them quickly degenerated into a simplistic, cost-benefit debate. For example, the Right To Die movement soon jettisoned its understandable concerns surrounding technologies that push individuals into allowing themselves to be slowly tortured to death by a "health" industry more obsessed with pursuing expensive research than with relieving suffering. The movement adopted instead the more simplistic debate that has some lives "worth more" to society than others.

Similarly, same-sex "marriage" and "civil unions" came to be more about invoking spousal-like benefits and legitimizing sexual license than anything to do with love. The abortion debate switched gears from "family planning" (a.k.a. birth control) and dealing with crimes like rape or incest, and instead began pursuing questions related to affordability, convenience and eugenics ("designer babies"). "Military intervention," formerly linked to the Nation's defense, suddenly became a euphemism for nation-building (or *appeasement*). We couldn't have war, you see, because wars kill people, resulting in feelings of guilt, and **Guilt Causes Neurosis**.

Thus did legislation enacted over the 30 years since Baby Boomers came of voting age come to differ less and less under either Democrats and Republicans. The rhetoric became a contest of slogans, thanks to a sound-bite-focused media obsessed with ratings. Whenever one administration would cut taxes or deregulate certain industries, the next would hike taxes and over-regulate to compensate for the previous administration's irresponsibility, and on and on, until the overall affect was more taxes, more intrusiveness and more unaccountability on the part of government.

Today, constitutional purists are out-maneuvered on issues ranging from social causes to the economy to national security, *even when their legislation passes*. "No deep thinking" has become the order of the day, for fear of being marginalized in the press and ridiculed by celebrities. To stay in power, a show of bipartisanship is made, under the misapprehension that elected (and unelected) officials are being "uniters instead of dividers" (to quote former President George W. Bush) or "merely being hired to give a speech" (to quote firebrand columnist Ann Coulter).

Such fears are not unfounded. Irrespective of party affiliation, everyone remembers what happened to successful 1990s talk show host, Laura Schlessinger (a.k.a. "Dr. Laura"), once on the brink of stardom with heavy support from TV sponsors, when she offered the tepid view (by today's standards) that homosexuality might be a "biological error," one which tended to be "predatory" when young boys are recruited. Immediately, the well-funded homosexual advocacy groups — the Gay & Lesbian Alliance Against Defamation (GLAAD) and the lesbian, gay, bisexual, and transsexual (LGBT) alliance, among others — went into overdrive, launching an online campaign, "StopDrLaura.com." The groups organized protests in 34 cities and pushed advertising boycotts directed personally at Dr. Schlessinger, not just her views, and tried to wreck both her existing radio program and a pending TV show she was about to host. Dr. Laura was characterized as a bigot, despite her earlier supportiveness of homosexual couples, as well as a youthful history of cohabitation, love affairs, nude photos and even a child conceived out of wedlock — all actions she later denounced once her views had "matured over time" (as per Thomas Paine) and she had adopted traditionalist principles.

Nevertheless, for her "biological error" and "predatory"

remarks, she went from being the second-highest-rated talk show host in America to virtual marginalization overnight, with zero tolerance for "thoughts that mature over time." On August 18, 2010, she announced she was quitting radio, despite a resurgence in her popularity, "to regain my First Amendment rights...[and] to say what is on my mind...."

In an exclusive interview with Newsmax, the renowned, if saucy and outspoken, radio host explained that the vicious attacks in the name of political correctness had taken away her First Amendment rights. "I've been through this as every...talk show [host] has a zillion times before," Dr. Laura said. "But somehow... after 32 years on radio, 17 [of them] syndicated...I sat down...and said 'I'm done trying to help people in a situation where my First Amendment rights don't exist, where special interest groups and activists can...silence you.' It's not American, it's not fair play.... It's bullying and it's scary. We're going in the direction of Russia because if you say the wrong thing you're toast."

Nothing is "comfortable" about these strong words, and Schlessinger hasn't been alone: College students at major universities across the country have been harassed and intimidated since before the year 2000. Adam Kissel, Director of the Individual Rights Defense Program, Foundation for Individual Rights in Education (FIRE), described in January 2008 a mandatory thought-reform program at the University of Delaware, aimed at some 7,000 students living in its dormitories. The school's Residence Life Staff — students given the sobriquet "Resident Assistant" (RA) — were specifically selected for their ideological views and then trained over the summer before class started. As RA's, they were assigned to question fellow resident-pupils on a variety of controversial issues, then assess their remarks and report back to school officials any allegedly incorrect thoughts, attitudes, values, and beliefs.

Similarities between the training and duties of the RA's and the old "Hitler's Youth" program are startling, as politically incorrect undergraduates are identified and reported on by fellow student-residents they would have no reason to suspect as being tools of a politically motivated alliance.

Another question surfaces in this debacle: How were the viewpoints and attitudes of these student recruits known beforehand? There had to be some hint beforehand, or else other collegiates and parents would have gotten wind of the program long before they did. The answer is that attitudinal data from middle-school and high-school surveys and questionnaires, which are often incorporated into "assessments" passed off as academic tests, probably were accessed. Psycho-political and sex questionnaires have been part and parcel of the pre-college experience since the 1980s, with student's responses going into databanks that can be accessed by any person or group, such as a college, with a "need to know." Responses are often graded, too, with personal queries rated on a scale of "preferred responses," the highest rating being known as a "minimum positive response." Nosy questionnaires cover everything from political controversies to drugs, race and sex. Pupils — and their parents — generally have little awareness concerning the extent to which "personal information" is being collected, stored and accessed, thereby making young collegiates easy marks for unethical recruitment as Resident Assistants (RA's).

Because the mission of FIRE is to defend and sustain individual rights at America's colleges and universities, the organization was alerted to the goings-on at the University of Delaware in a complaint by a student's father. His freshman son had described to him a coordinated strategy of coercive, mandatory activities in his dormitory, which the boy viewed as "ugly, hateful, and extremely divisive." He said that the program forced students "to act out the worst possible racial stereotypes and was replete with...ideological Commentary and gratuitous slurs...."

Nothing comfortable there!

After FIRE investigated — and put some 500 pages of documentation online — the public outcry ended a so-called "Diversity Facilitation Training" program, for the time being. Later, it was discovered that other colleges and universities had (and still have) similar programs. Mr. Kissel says these are "a comprehensive manipulation of the living environment to inculcate, unrelentingly, the ideological views insisted upon by the university's Residence Life Staff. It is telling that one administrator described the point of the exercise as leaving 'a mental footprint on [a pupil's] consciousness'."

Such programs obviously are put in place to keep a youngish "Dr. Laura"-type of collegiate from bursting onto the national scene. Forgotten in this logic is the fact that if *one* side can get away with such manipulation, so can its opposite number, somewhere down the road. The fact that indoctrination and intimidation of thought is now justified at major institutions runs completely counter to the ideal of free conscience and would have the Nation's Founders turning over in their graves.

Nevertheless, coercion of thought continues to filter down, earning less than a shoulder shrug by both major political parties. Such manipulation also pervades government agencies — usually via mandatory workshops for employees concerning sexual-harassment, diversity, sexual tolerance, and race and other hot-button topics. So, while local mayors work to oust Santa Clause (because the figure is associated with a Christian holiday)[6] via neighborhood-based "town hall" style meetings, New York City is asked to countenance a mosque near Ground Zero. The Air Conditioning Contractors of America (ACCA) communication director, Melissa Broadus, revealed in a post on October 20, 1010 (as did other sources like the *Wall Street Journal* and *The Washington Times*) that in California utility companies tasked analysts (probably psychologists with experience in statistics) with "studying the impact of peer pressure on energy consumption by including information in monthly bills that compares customers' electricity use with that of their neighbors. Not

---

[6]   In Nov.-Dec., 2001, Mayor Lynn Raufaste of Kensington, MD, tried unsuccessfully to ban Santa Claus from making its annual rounds of on a mobile stage featuring children in holiday costumes, choral singing, decorations and, of course, Santa's famous ho-ho-ho. The brouhaha drew national media attention.

surprisingly, carbon shame works...."[7] Bigwigs like House Speaker Nancy Pelosi (D-CA)no doubt would not be included in such "peer pressure" studies. In neighborhood settings, individuals are similarly pressured using alternative strategies like the Delphi Technique, the Tavistock Method, and Saul Alinsky's tactics of "community organization."

Unbelievably, in just 25 years America's open society, which prided itself on freedom of thought, has become a bullying conglomerate that insists everyone be "on the same page," or suffer the discomforting loss of livelihood, status and reputation.

The future of the Republic as the Founders envisioned it appears dismal indeed. Nothing short of a massive uprising may be able, at this juncture, to reverse the course toward outright regimentation. Such an approach is itself risky, as massive uprisings too often lead to anarchy and violence, which then, of course, must be smashed by an equally virulent government. When that happens, a nation typically falls under some sort of martial law, and then moves quickly to a "police state."

That is why the current sprints toward *uber*-regulation, government takeovers, and supervision of authority by international entities comprise the overriding threats facing Americans, and also the most misunderstood. Increasingly, a Nanny State is being superimposed surreptitiously onto the Nation's legal structure and embedded into our country's most trusted

---

[7]   See: "Carbon Shame Goes Global," *Washington Times* editorial, Oct. 22, 2010.

institutions — schools, youth associations, financial institutions and even some religious organizations. Big Government is propagandized through entertainment venues, from TV dramas and movies to cartoons and video games — often deliberately, but sometimes not: almost as if propagandists themselves can't tell the difference.

Foreign organizations, many of them cast as international, humanitarian groups or alliances — ostensibly to support education and "awareness" — figure highly in this subterfuge. For example, Socialist International (SI) is one of the world's most influential organizations. It pushes both worldwide socialism as the most reliable form of governance, as well as international oversight of sovereign nations, yet SI is virtually unknown to Americans and is rarely mentioned in the media. And SI is by no means alone.

How can people *not* know? One answer, again, is "information overload," a byproduct of the quantum leap in communications technology and the digital age. The fact that SI's website ran headline stories from the end of December 2009 through January 2010 highlighting the organization's influence at the United Nations Climate Change Summit in Copenhagen, Denmark, even as it openly advocated a buildup in *militant*, global, environmental-lobbying efforts, exemplifies the level of public cluelessness when it comes to influence-peddling. There is simply so much information out there that the average American cannot even begin to keep up with it. Our news media, even the rigorous journalists, are overwhelmed.

Too often, the challenges to our way of life are emanating from sources that, technically, are outside of the Nation's borders. These sources are well-subsidized, with tentacles that extend to the highest levels of our government and its agencies. Foreign entities manipulate our media, influence government officials and corporate policies, proselytize through school curriculum, promote their agendas from television and magazine ads, and compromise our military.

The ongoing nature of this situation necessarily diminishes the Nation's sovereignty and the authority of average citizens, until the individual vote is stripped of meaning, substituting a false sense of empowerment. In reality, America's mainstream populace is dangerously close to the point where it wields *no* authority and officials cannot be held accountable in any substantive way.

Moreover, the parallels between 1774, 1939 and 2010 are eerily similar — proving, once again, that while the faces, names and exact nature of various power grabs may change, the unchecked use of power by egotistical and self-serving elites is constant. Human nature, it seems, does not change, after all.

With a nuclear Middle East on the horizon; another financial collapse waiting to happen; once-noble ideals and traditions undermined on a daily basis; a so-called environmental movement determined to utilize "energy" as a new means of wealth redistribution; and a burgeoning surveillance society boasting ever-more-sophisticated (and expensive) gadgetry with which to regiment individuals, this doesn't seem to be a good time to lay back and "get comfortable."

Section 2.- **CATEGORIZING AMERICA'S MOST PRESSING ISSUES**

The sheer number of urgent and controversial issues we face as we approach the general election in 2012 requires a systematized approach.   Set out below in outline form are America's most pressing issues.   Some, of course, overlap, and all carry the overriding concern that our constitutional republic is being phased out to make room for world government.   Since the majority of the world's governments are socialistic, it requires no great leap of imagination to believe we are being pushed into that mold as well.

Therefore, the following outline serves as a basis for discussion and reference: the sections titled "Abuses and Usurpations" and "The Platform" will be cross-matched with the outline below, using the numerical codes preceding each itemized issue (1a, 2b, etc...) to show their respective connections and interrelationships.

1. Constitutional Powers
- 1a. **Party System, Funding and Representation**
- 1b. **Separation of Powers and Checks and Balances**
- 1c. **Legislative Process**

Transportation

9a.   **Crumbling Infrastructure**

9b.   **Alternative Energy Development**

9c.   **Medical Research**

10. Environment[8]

10a.   **Property Rights vs. *Sustainable Communities***

10b.   **Public Lands and Resources**

10c.   **Energy Rights and Public Policy**

11. Education[9]

11a.   **U.S. Dept. of Education and State/local agencies**

11b.   **Private vs. Public Options**

11c.   **Teacher Education, Unions & U.N. Influence**

11d.   **Federal vs. Local Control**

11e.   **Assimilation Tool for Legal Immigrants**

A Note on the Inter-Relationships Affecting the Departments of Energy and Education:

The Environmental Protection Agency and the U.S. Department of Education, two of the most corrupt bureaucracies in government, need to be shut down. Doing so will be problematic at this point, as hundreds

---

[8]   See "A Note on the Inter-Relationship Affecting the Departments of Energy and Education," beneath this outline.

[9]   See "A Note on the Inter-Relationship Affecting the Departments of Energy and Education," beneath this outline.

of vested interests, mostly uninterested in either the environment or education per se, stand to benefit from their policies and *diktats*, which of course can be safely circumvented only by multimillionaires. Both agencies are related in that only the failure of the education system could have produced a populace ignorant enough to fall for frauds like "global warming," "global climate disruption," (or whatever the term *dujour* for it happens to be).

"Global warming" (and its predecessor, "global cooling") probably are the mothers of all scams, along with the nonsense about "carbon footprints." Both concepts utilize phony science to redistribute the wealth of average people, redistribution being the whole point of socialism. Worse, however, the climate con is contributing to violence along the U.S.-Mexican border, posing an additional national security risk, as detailed in a report spearheaded by Rep. Rob Bishop (R-Utah) and 11 other members of the House and Senate. The Department of Energy, fixated as usual on relatively unimportant "endangered" life forms (in this case the ocelot in Texas and the Sonoron pronghorn in Arizona), both of them along a 32-mile desert wasteland that comprises a short portion of the border. The Department's position is aiding and abetting not only illegal immigration but prospective terrorists, who can count on an absence of helicopter surveillance along that particular stretch. Never mind that average Americans are meanwhile removing their shoes, being patted down and suffering all manner of ridiculous indignities at the Nation's airports, while government agencies relinquish the responsibility of security along 32 miles of border-land.

Aside from the inclusion of "junk science" into our children's curricula, with the blessing of the U.S. Department of Education (and its state clones and predecessor, the old Office of Education under the U.S. Department of Health, Education and Welfare), this agency has caused a precipitously lowering of the level of knowledge overall and turned the atmosphere of educational facilities into killing fields at which young people are warehoused and psychologized, but not educated. Subjects like history and health are today laughable shadows of their former selves under banners like Social Studies and Sex Education. Even the most broadminded parents admit that their children and grandchildren are not half as well-schooled (or as mature, given their level of dependency) as themselves at the same age and grade level.

The political will to shut down these agencies will not, and indeed cannot, at this point reside with the major political parties, because they are beholden to foundations, associations, institutes and organizations that serve as their benefactors (Greenpeace and the Sierra Club come to mind). Both agencies are too far gone to be simply retooled, so constituents should not rely on promises by candidates to reform either agency. Shutting down the Departments of Energy and Education will have to come from the People, which may be a good place to draw a line in the sand, serving notice to officials that government works for us, not the other

way around. This could well become a first test of the
People's might and their mettle.

Section 3.- A WORD ON JEFFERSON'S "ABUSES AND USURPATIONS"

States' rights and individual citizens have suffered for some 40 years at the hands of a burgeoning federal bureaucracy, a compromised judiciary and an overbearing, careerist Legislative Branch. Initiated under President Woodrow Wilson along with his brainstorm, the League of Nations, successive assaults on American liberties accelerated under the presidency of Franklin Delano Roosevelt, who used the dual emergencies of the Great Depression and World War II to vastly strengthen Federal Government. Since that time, abuses have trickled down to the Nation's states, counties and vital institutions (like schools) through mandates, directives and executive orders conceived in Washington, DC, and also by the use of monetary incentives from government agencies serving as "carrots" to extend federal control.

The result today is a sprint to "the finish line" with yet another wave of career radicals leading the charge toward a burgeoning tyranny. Their justification is that the Constitution which the Framers produced is outdated and no longer workable. A four-pronged strategy, therefore, is aimed at finishing the job: vast increases in the number of regulations, red tape, surveillance and paperwork.

The negative spinoffs emanating from thousands of pages of new federal mandates have not stopped with state, county or city governments. All of North America is now affected to the point where the real needs of local constituents are not protected. The most glaring example is the virtual invasion at our southern border from waves of outlaws ranging from violent drug cartels and the Russian mafia to Taliban-Al Qaeda spy cells and military combatants. Still others merely want access to American benefits, salaries and goods, but do not wish to assimilate or wait their turn so that their immigration can proceed in an organized fashion.

The result is a free-for-all. State and local law enforcement are actually prevented from protecting their citizens because of federal regulations that either pre-empt or conflict with longstanding local laws. So emboldened have the competing factions of various outlaws become that they often murder at random border-state residents who own homes, land and cattle and then take up residence on their land, which serves as a kind of "safe house" for criminal activity. This is a new and unprecedented weakness in our national defense and security is not being addressed.

Americans have patiently suffered at the hands of a political caste whose members no longer feel any particular sense of loyalty to their constituents or, for that matter, to America. This superior attitude extends to political appointees and career bureaucrats serving in top jobs, having assumed their coveted positions via any one of hundreds of foundations, associations, big corporations and institutes that make it their business to wine and dine, "aid and abet" the governing caste.

Take Thomas R. Nides, a six-figure fundraiser for Hillary Clinton's 2008 presidential bid, who also just happened to have made a considerable fortune as chief operating officer for Morgan Stanley, one of the global financial service firms that received (and, to its credit, repaid) federal bailout money. But he also received more than $8 million in salary and bonuses and was eligible for even more at the time he was tapped for Deputy Secretary of State in the fall of 2010. And guess who Mr. Nides was replacing: Jacob Lew, a gentleman awaiting confirmation as federal budget chief on the one hand, and some $1 million on the other — from bailed-out banking giant, Citigroup, no less.[10]

This is not to single out one particular administration or person, as most administrations in recent memory have tapped people of similar means for top posts. The point is that the whole ethic about "avoiding any appearance of impropriety" has gone with the wind. Actual scandals involving household-name public servants grace the pages of newspapers and online news services on a nearly weekly basis, yet they receive a "slap on the wrist" for things that would land the average taxpayers in prison. What this means is that most of the people running the government are so far removed

---

[10] "Wall St. mogul picked for State post," by Jim McElhatton, *The Washington Times*, Oct. 12, 2010, p. A-1.

from the plight of average taxpayers that no comparison is even possible.

It is incumbent upon the American populace, therefore, to speedily set a corrective course (preferably before some foreign entity does it for us, by force), and replace what has become an unresponsive, arrogant governing caste with individuals whose *first* allegiance is to "We, the People." That was the essence of Thomas Jefferson's List of Abuses and Usurpations in 1776, and it is the essence of the matter now, in 2010.

Section 4.- **SUMMARY LIST OF ABUSES AND USURPATIONS, CIRCA 2010**

What follows is "a long train of abuses and usurpations," to quote Thomas Jefferson in the Declaration of Independence. This Section itemizes the most grievous failings of our "hyperactive" United States Government — outright abuses, blatant takeovers and power grabs via a system of aligned and partnering agencies that work hand-in-hand with federal agencies as well as the three branches of government. Some were established directly and funded, such as the Council of Chief State School Officers; others emerged as a result of tax incentives, grants, contracts and unfunded mandates. Please note that all entries below are cross-matched to the corresponding categories outlined in the Section 2. Many of the listings below necessarily intersect with, or touch on, two or more categories; thus, the frequent use of more than one reference tag.

➢ Whereas the established political parties, as they exist in the year 2010, have outlived their usefulness; nor is a Party system specifically endorsed by the U.S. Constitution as a method of selecting candidates for public office... (1a)

➢ Whereas the salaries, "perks" and benefits of elected representatives and officials are at levels that fail to represent a median compensation for comparable work in the private sector (e.g., pensions and health plans go on indefinitely after they leave office), thereby creating a governing caste that is overly removed from the citizenry, excessively process-oriented, and frivolous in its expenditures (e.g., travel, "fact-finding" trips, etc.) ... (1a)

➢ Whereas the U.S. political system has vastly accelerated its move away from the Founding notion that governments "derive their just powers from the consent of the governed," a clear symptom being the disinterest on the part of candidates in disseminating comparative information packets on the issues of interest to registered voters prior to an election time... (1b, 1d))

➢ Whereas the Constitution of the United States is the foundation upon which our federal government was constructed, not a loose document to be bypassed or re-interpreted, but one that was to endure in perpetuity and amended, as events dictated, only through the process prescribed by the Framers... (1b)

➢ Whereas the rationale behind the election of representatives was conceived to ensure that a management of government by proxy did not occur, as well as to uphold and defend the "unalienable rights" of legal citizens under the Declaration of Independence... (1c, 2a)

➢ Whereas any remaining powers not specifically delegated by the Constitution to the federal government automatically default back *to the people*, **not** to either federal or state governments (save for limited exceptions, such as the negotiation of international treaties)... (1b)

➢ Whereas Executive Orders usurp the functions of Congress and even the Supreme Court, in an attempt to circumvent the U.S. Constitution and its system of checks and balances...(1b)

➢ Whereas the 50 States are losing both their individuality and their rightful prerogatives to an overbearing federal government via a system of "cloned" agencies, not to mention grants, contracts and "partnerships" beholden to bureaucracies thousands of miles away, is compromising state sovereignty and bypassing the Constitution, state legislatures and the courts... (1d)

➢ Whereas the legislative process has become polluted via the addition of unrelated "earmarks" and "riders," usually to satisfy a pet project or special interest, or to otherwise gain support for an unpopular bill... (1c)

➢ Whereas Political Correctness increasingly erodes the constitutional right to free speech, freedom of assembly, thought and conscience, under various deceptive monikers (e.g., "fairness doctrine," "hate speech"), thereby compromising essential tools bequeathed citizens by this nation's Founders... (1e)

➢ Whereas the Second Amendment to the U.S. Constitution (the right to keep and bear arms) was conceived as a means of personal self-protection as well as to serve as a check against oppressive or tyrannical government, safeguarding life, liberty and personal property... (1f)

➢ Whereas all three branches of government have undertaken a 35-year effort to twist the "Establishment Clause" into a call for eradicating religious expression, especially certain Christianity-inspired elements of our Constitution, even though the Framers clearly limited their assertions to a commitment that religion remain free of mandated sectarianism and coercion (to attend services, etc.)... (2d, 4d, 1e)

➢ Whereas the values of self-sufficiency, self-determination and independence (which undergird the U.S. Constitution, the Bill of Rights and the Declaration of Independence) receive lip-service, the dependency-collectivist model is the one favored by the United Nations and its ardent supporters, thereby strengthening a Big Government mindset, meddling (ineffectively) in the affairs of nations, and "partnering" with agencies that end up serving as proxies outside any system of checks-and-balances... (2a, 3c)

➢ Whereas the American form of government, as created by its Founders, is not a pure democracy, but a *republic*, which carries distinct advantages:

a body of fixed and objective laws not as subject to whim and societal experimentation, whether by an organized lobby, Congress or the Judiciary... (2a)

➤ Whereas the Framers made it clear, in letters to each other while drafting the U.S. Constitution (e.g., "Federalist Papers"), that "pure" democracies too easily devolve into mob rule, anarchy and tyranny and, therefore, are incompatible with long-term personal prosperity, security and property rights... (2a)

➤ Whereas the term "democracy" appears nowhere in the Declaration of Independence, in the U.S. Constitution or its predecessor, the Articles of Confederation, or in any of the State constitutions...(2a)

➤ Whereas, wars aimed at appeasing and making "friends" of our enemies abroad, instead of being launched only in the interests of our defense and national security, are costing thousands of American lives, for little, if any, benefit, while seditious acts — notably Shariah-compliant financial structures and tenets that are incompatible with the civil liberties enshrined in the U.S. Constitution are being promoted at home... (3c, 4a, 2a)

➤ Whereas the imperative of the Declaration of Independence to support the individual's "pursuit of happiness" is being subtly retooled into an imperative to *guarantee* happiness... (3a, 5d)

➤ Whereas the U.S. Territories, like illegal immigrants, enjoy many of the same taxpayer-subsidized benefits as do taxpayers in the States... (3b)

➤ Whereas over the past 30 years, enormous license has been taken with respect to the 14th Amendment, which is now presumed to give birthright citizenship to the children of illegal residents born in the U.S.; and whereas the U.S. Supreme Court has yet to determine the meaning of the clause "subject to jurisdiction thereof" or to define the requirements of allegiance ("ligiance of her Majesty," as stipulated in original writings relating to birthright citizenship) ... (4c)

➤ Whereas billions of dollars are spent on foreign aid (humanitarian and otherwise), at little or no benefit to average citizens, thereby encouraging a policy of blackmail on the part of tyrannical leaders... (4a)

➤ Whereas, a dubiously funded, religiously based "cultural center" is being given a green light on the basis of religious freedom at the site of the worst attack upon our nation in its history, in effect honoring foreign combatants... (4a, 4d)

➤ Whereas granting foreign nationals (a.k.a. "terrorists," "combatants") who commit destructive attacks against Americans and their properties are being awarded the same civilian rights as legal citizens under the Nation's criminal justice code, as opposed being handed over to the military for arraignment, thereby providing a podium for terrorist propaganda and further clogging civilian courts... (4b)

➢ Whereas this nation was created largely out of European immigrants, today's influx of illegal residents — without benefit of sponsorship, employment or intent to assimilate — now threatens to unravel America's financial stability, safety, security, ideals, education, traditions and the "general welfare," as that term is defined by the U.S. Constitution... (4c)

➢ Whereas waves of illegal and often unemployable immigrants — untutored in the English language, uncommitted to American ideals, *illiterate even in their native lands*, ignorant of the founding documents along with the rights and responsibilities contained therein, and having no understanding of what any U.S. candidate or political party stands for — have been granted citizenship for the sole purpose of awarding the office-seeker ill-gotten votes...(4c, 11f)

➢ Whereas failure to designate English as the official language of the United States, and to ensure that every immigrant demonstrates a comprehensible level of proficiency prior to citizenship and long-term residency, damages national security... (4c, 4d)

➢ Whereas overt bigotry by individual Americans and their institutions is on the wane, federal and state governments (including tax-supported educational facilities) have redoubled their efforts to pander to particularism under the guise of "multiculturalism" and "diversity," exacerbating racism and producing an inevitable backlash, both of which undermine national security...(4d, 11f)

➤ Whereas American expressions of traditional family life are afforded less legitimacy than the rants of counterculture groups and criminals... (4d, 5c)

➤ Whereas, federal subsidies (or tax exemptions) to radical and extremist groups — e.g., ACORN,[11] Greenpeace, the American Civil Liberties Union, The Muslim Brotherhood, etc. — allow infiltrators and criminals to operate surreptitiously, twisting constitutional ideals and wasting American tax dollars...(4e, 6c)

➤ Whereas a cadre so-called environmental groups (some of them foreign) have been allowed to dictate legislation supporting fraudulent claims, requiring acquiescence to "junk science" as a condition of continued agency funding, impairing realistic energy research, food production and legitimate infrastructure needs...(4e, 9b)

➤ Whereas calls by the Speaker of the House and other government officials to investigate "resisters" to programs deemed in the interests of the governing caste (e.g., the mosque and "cultural center" at Ground Zero in New York City) ...(6c, 2b)

---

[11]   Association of Community Organizations for Reform Now.

➤ Whereas the criminal justice system increasingly fails to protect citizens from ever-more-grisly incidences of violent crime and intimidation from criminals with long "rap sheets" (it costs more to execute violent, career criminals than it does to keep them in the prisons or parole them ... (5b)

➤ Whereas incarcerated criminals, rather than working to support their upkeep in self-sustaining prisons, are instead being fully subsidized (food, shelter, medical care, recreation) at taxpayer expense, with little or no restitution expected even from the worst offenders (who often spend their prison time spreading sexually transmitted diseases and writing letters to government agencies to complain about conditions), the criminal justice system is sowing general disrespect for law enforcement... (5b)

➤ Whereas tax dollars are being wasted on petty "crimes" (e.g., "click-it-or-ticket" stops, "traffic" cameras that exacerbate accidents, bicycle-helmet fines, etc.) and which serve no purpose other than revenue enhancement, and overregulation ("*uber-criminalization*") generates disrespect for the law and the police... (5c)

➤ Whereas the tsunami of newer and pending technologies over the past two decades has revolutionized not only communications and collection of personal data, but has made individuals, institutions and the secret ballot vulnerable, often unknowingly, to illegal probes by private and governmental entities (domestic and foreign) for political and/or illicit purposes... (5c, 5d)

➤ Whereas a cottage industry of mental health activists is teaming with the pharmaceutical industry to normalize use of mind-altering ("psychotropic") substances, many former patients are now suspected of complicity in horrific crimes... (5c, 8c, 9c)

➤ Whereas controversial therapies for "diseases" that lack any means of definitive testing nevertheless continue unchecked... (8c, 9c)

➤ Whereas a program of government snooping under the cover of "data collection" continues unabated, even for such trivialities as a citizen's online book selections...(5d)

➤ Whereas terrorism and other incursions by foreign entities (whether it be a faction/group or a established country/power) constitute an Act of War and, therefore, a threat to national security ... (6a)

➤ Whereas Congress cannot apparently distinguish between a Declaration of War and a "Police Action"...(6b)

➤ Whereas those responsible for our national security spend more effort inconveniencing and harassing upstanding citizens than securing the borders...

➤ Whereas the inflationary practice by the U.S. Treasury of printing unsecured notes devalues the

Nation's currency and is incompatible with a free-market economy... (7a)

- ➢ Whereas "free trade" has become a one-way street in which other nations trade freely with *us* and pocket the benefits, and America manufactures and produces relatively little at home and increasingly exports its jobs overseas... (7a)

- ➢ Whereas the federal government, under guise of "saving" our beleaguered economy, has rushed to "bail out," at taxpayers' expense, private corporations, businesses and other large institutions that are deemed "too big to fail," thereby creating the conditions for nationalization, federalization and over-regulation — all hallmarks of a totalitarian state... (7b)

- ➢ Whereas Big Government is undermining the principle of a free-market economy and its accompanying profit motive via overregulation, compromising the Nation's productivity, high standard of living and political stability... (7b)

- ➢ Whereas an increasingly centralized and regulated economic model has created an "entitlement culture," undermining the original intent of unfettered free enterprise, as articulated under the Framers' model, and fails to reward merit and hard work, or to protect the ideals of private ownership, risk-and-reward, industriousness, competition, investment-and-return... (7c, 2b)

- Whereas the cost to private entities of hiring workers is often prohibitive due to overregulation — workers' compensation, unemployment and health insurance, secure record-keeping (such as Social Security data), environmental/safety regulations, business regulations (every purchase over $600 requires a 1099 form, which in turn requires another part-time or full-time employee to obtain the address, insurance company and tax ID information from companies providing bulk purchases, like an office-supply store)... (7e)

- Whereas a systematic course of over-obligating taxpayer funds threatens to bring the Nation to a financial standstill... (7f)

- Whereas taxes are at an all-time high, and "soak-the-rich" schemes have filtered down to include upper-middle-class households, stifling entrepreneurship and job creation...(7f)

- Whereas failure of both Federal and State governments to cease reckless spending, waste and inflationary monetary practices creating the conditions for eventual insolvency... (7f)

- Whereas the present health care system is not serving Americans well for reasons either not addressed, or mischaracterized under current and proposed health-care reform initiatives, among them (8a, b, c):

  o expensive new technologies that ignore quality-of-life issues;

- pressure upon physicians to pursue expensive, exceedingly painful, experimental options with the threat of family members being charged with medical negligence;

- artificially created shortages of doctors as a consequence of medical school admission policies;

- a precipitous decline in post-graduate course work, recordkeeping, and cross-training, leading to unjustifiable mistakes;

- frivolous lawsuits (many of which can be traced back to government, the over-production of lawyers, and case law that permits outsized judgments);

- scam peer reviews and a pharmacology industry that lacks integrity;

- health-insurance companies that cover little but charge high premiums to satisfy investors and government regulators, without allowance for open competition across state lines;

- hospital emergency rooms that are bound by government fiat to treat non-emergencies and which delivers preferential care to indigents and illegal aliens over legal citizens *with* insurance and life-threatening illnesses to avoid the appearance of "discrimination";

- drug-enforcement policies that deny needed medications to those who need them while leaving real criminals and addicts unscathed; and

- "privacy" regulations that discourage family involvement (and information) and leave incapacitated patients in the lurch...

➢ Whereas federal regulation and oversight of drugs is overly focused on "recreational" and illegal substances to the detriment of the Nation's pre-1970s standard, which ensured that lethal and debilitating legal medications were not allowed to go to market until they had been thoroughly tested for safety... (9c)

➢ Whereas the 119-mile-long Suez Canal, which connects the Mediterranean Sea and the Red Sea, was constructed in just 10 years in the mid-1850s, without modern technologies now taken for granted, whereas construction of a 35-mile-long stretch of road today[12] takes as long as 50 years ...(9a)

➢ Whereas the misuse and outright abuse of so-called environmental stewardship has resulted in fraudulent and often outright illegal legislation under a variety of ruses (e.g., the Environmental Protection Act, the Endangered Species Act, the Clean Water Act, "sustainable development," "conservation," etc.), all committed to advancing a policy of wealth redistribution ... (10a, 10b)

➢ Whereas 40 years of government-subsidized propaganda via the Nation's teacher training institutions and K-12 schools has inculcated young Americans with an entitlement mindset, so

---

[12] e.g., the Fairfax, Virginia, County Parkway

that a brainwashed public now expects government to provide taxpayer-supplied breakfasts, lunches, snacks, transportation, pensions, health care and a guaranteed income... (11c)

➢ Whereas the taxpayer-subsidized education system no longer emphasizes (and even pointedly disregards) the Declaration of Independence, the Federalist Papers and the U.S. Constitution while spending inordinate amounts of time on "model United Nations" projects ... (11c)

➢ Whereas the government's virtual monopoly over education, including teacher training, has eroded educational priorities, advanced "junk science," maligned parents and held private-schooling options in contempt (except for the elite and the ruling caste)... (11b, 11c)

...Therefore, the legal citizens of these United States do hereby insist upon a profound adjustment to the status quo and a rectifying course of action, articulated in rational Platform that is centered on the core American values of Fiscal Responsibility, Constitutionally Limited Government, Free Markets and Free Conscience, all operating in an environment of integrity, principled decency and self-control.

Section 5.- **WHAT AMERICANS WANT:**

Tenets Underlying a Rational, Modern-Day Platform

Any attempt to compose a rational, Common Sense Platform must be built around a set of guiding tenets, or guidelines. These include:

Fiscal Responsibility: The freedom of the individual to keep money that is the fruit of one's own labor. *Fiscal responsibility* means government at all levels being held to a budget, comprised of needs that citizens have actually approved, either via referendum or their elected representatives. Failure to construct and live within an annual budget, and failure of elected representatives to articulate clearly both the fixed and operational costs of potential expenditures, and to win constituents' approval of the same, is a recipe for progressively higher levels of taxation, out-of-control spending and a government bureaucracy that exists to serve itself. Runaway deficit spending, such as presently exists, compels American citizens to take back the purse strings and tell their elected representatives what they do and do not want to pay for.

Constitutionally Limited Government: As articulated in America's founding documents, including the published deliberations between the Framers, the Constitution of the United States is the supreme law of the land, written in plain language so as be comprehensible to future generations. In that vein, states' rights are preserved, and powers not expressly given to the federal government by the U.S. Constitution default back to the people, thereby enhancing the liberty of the individual within the rule of law.

Free Markets: A market-based economy is the only ethical form of commerce, based as it is on the individual right to the fruit of one's own labors and the liberty to pursue a career which best fits a person's own interests and intelligence. A closed, government-regulated economy is the antithesis of liberty; for it produces favoritism, creates unemployment, reduces risk and incentive, and perpetuates a self-aggrandizing bureaucracy which, in turn, creates a vicious cycle of increased government. Government interference into the operations of private businesses cannot be tolerated, unless such intervention is specifically required by the U.S. Constitution in the interests of the Nation's sovereignty, defense, or individual rights (i.e., human trafficking and other offenses that constitute an illegal action). *The term "free-market socialism" is the most onerous oxymoron of our times.*

An Environment of Integrity, Principled Decency and Self-Control (*or, a note concerning the role of religion in public life*): Any unbiased reading of the Founders' letters and other writings carries a presumption of "general Christianity," a term specifically used by Thomas Jefferson in the "Virginia Act for Establishing Religious Freedom" (but rarely cited in its full context today), to denote the prevailing ethical basis of the colonies-*cum*-states at that time. Jefferson's position is further reinforced by John Adams: *"Our Constitution is designed only for a moral and religious people. It is wholly inadequate for any other...."* Other statements and writings, taken together, acknowledge a set of ideals, the underpinnings of which comprise the extensive liberties and freedoms unique to the United States. In countries where these ideals are either unknown or otherwise not included as part of the rationale for a governing national document, the nation has not thrived.

Much of what is contained in the U.S. Constitution and the Bill of Rights is rooted in an assumption that all citizens are "children of the Almighty God," in the Christian tradition, along with other enhancements from Greek and Roman philosophy. This helped diminish mankind's less civilized urges and put the brakes on decadent conduct, while still allowing for difference in specific religious affiliation. When we took Bible readings and prayer out of schools we did two things: We removed a set of principles which cost us taxpayers nothing and served as a reminder to children that there was Something higher than their own greed who was watching; and we installed metal detectors, surveillance cameras, a constant police presence and teams of psychiatrists, which cost taxpayers a whole lot, but accomplished nothing.

The Founders' ruminations on religious expression contain many references to self-control, adherence to principle, high integrity — among various references to Christ, who was held up as the supreme example of what the Founders thought of as good citizenship. Forgotten in the debate over Christianity's influence is something Thomas Jefferson noticed and described: "[Y]et he chose not to propagate it by coercions...." Therein lies the key to the role of religion in America: non-coercive, but there all the same.

There is no way, in the above context, that the so-called "Establishment Clause" could be interpreted as a means of "making room" for other faiths by eradicating other religious tenets. Rather, the Clause is seen as *nourishing* the *prevailing* religious ideals, values that were already part and parcel of the fledgling Nation's majority ethical and cultural heritage. One can still see the original, ornate Christian frescos adorning the ceilings and walls of grand historical buildings, such as the State House in Harrisburg, Pennsylvania. Jefferson also alluded to not falling into the trap of "beget[ting] habits of hypocrisy and meanness..." as had been the practice of so many other governments throughout the Old World.

The Framers' key position, then, with regard to the relationship of religion and government, was "non-coercion." The only way in which a people would be successful at self-rule was deemed to be in an atmosphere of non-coercion, **_but_** with the caveat of self-control and personal responsibility, which the Framers apparently viewed as by-products of a Christian outlook.

Minus self-control and personal responsibility, the Constitution, as John Adams put it, would be "wholly inadequate," along with any concepts about self-reliance, self-determination, self-sufficiency and so on. Thus, the post-1960s attempt to eradicate religious tenets has led to moral turpitude, dependency, and civil disobedience. We have virtually toppled the Nation's moral and ethical underpinnings — the very glue that holds together the experiment in self-rule. This will result in a society that implodes under the weight of its own corruption, crises and chaos.

Thus, the significance and relationship of religion to self-government, *in the Framers' view*, was the establishment what we would call today a "default setting," a climate in which integrity, principled decency and self-control are the *norm*, allowing for the kinds of political deliberations and active participation characteristic of a non-coercive style, free of intimidation and cruelty, which are the only ways that self-government can work. Recent attempts to replace *this* climate, to strip away *these* norms by imposing political correctness, regimentation and *uber*-regulation reflect an attempt to curtail free conscience, thought and expression, and by extension, religious freedom as well. This is an atmosphere in which self-government cannot, and will not, thrive.

In view of all these factors, Americans want to see:

- Restoration of the Founding principles to government — primary among them being a constitutionally supported system of *ethics*; a vastly reduced bureaucracy, and an end to wasteful expenditures and red tape;

- Reinstatement of free-market principles, with a policy of non-interference by government entities;

- Loyalty to the founding principle of private property rights and individual ownership;

- Commitment to the supremacy of the individual over the collective (i.e., and concomitant discouragement of mob rule);

- Encouragement of free information flow concerning issues and candidates;

- Reversal of the entitlement (welfare) mentality, including all redistributions-of-wealth schemes;

- Re-establishment of merit and work as the currency of success, together with concomitant values of self-sufficiency and self-reliance as the currencies of upward mobility;

- Restoration of firm budgetary constraints;

- Re-dedication to *American* industry, manufacturing, and workforce, as opposed to unbridled globalization, "outsourcing" and "importation";

- Restoration of key ideals like states' rights, private property and individual ownership, hard work, excellence and discipline in our nation's classrooms;

- Cessation of wealth-redistribution schemes, under whatever deceptive moniker (e.g., "Sustainable Development," "Livable Communities," "Full-Service Education," "Cap-and-Trade," etc...);

- De-emphasis on tax-supported foreign aid, "humanitarian" or otherwise, and encouragement of local charities and private organizations to provide voluntary assistance;

- Denial of aid to regimes/causes that are overtly hostile to American values;

- Re-activation of *sponsorship* as a condition of immigration;

- Commitment to long-term energy independence, for which the Nation's space and nuclear research programs have already laid the groundwork;

- Across-the-board rejection of sloppy or fraudulent science that funds politically correct dogma (e.g., "global cooling," "global warming," "man-made climate change," "population time-bomb," "bipolar disorder," "attention-deficit disorder," etc...) and punishment for (de-funding of) entities that *knowingly* advance falsehoods for political or monetary gain;

- Suspension of government involvement with, and tax support for radical front organizations (e.g., ACORN and the ACLU[13]);

- Top-to-bottom overhaul of law enforcement and criminal justice so that they once again warrant the respect of responsible citizens;

- Neighborhoods in which parents can let children out of doors to play like they used to, meaning living environments with real, not phony, "community policing," with unmarked police cars seeking specifically kidnappers and sex offenders that target children at play and at bus stops, as well as court systems (including judges) that make it their mission to focus on **truly** violent predators; and

- Re-commitment to free speech in a digital age without caving to prurient interest groups, such as Internet pornographers.

---

[13] The American Civil Liberties Union specializes in quasi-mandatory *pro bono* legal work by young, usually new attorneys (i.e., as a condition of future recommendations for employment) that frequently promotes causes that run contrary to U.S. principles and twists the Founders' words. Pressure to take on a case is very hard to prove.

Section 6.- **THE PLATFORM**

In light of the above guiding tenets, the following rational, Common Sense Platform sets out these positions:

With a Party system now thoroughly corroded by scandals, a cottage industry of professional "handlers" and "consultants" that specializes in strategic manipulation, and a political process tainted through hidden (and sometimes foreign) billionaires who bankroll both candidates and lobbying efforts, an overhaul of the electoral process is necessary to re-activate an increasingly unrepresented and alienated American populace. (1a)

The Constitution of the United States remains the foundation upon which government is constructed, not as a loose document to be circumvented, bypassed or "updated" as if were a set of annual organization plans, but as intended: in perpetuity, amended only (as events dictate) through the process prescribed by the Framers. (1b)

Potential candidates, as well as existing leaders at the local, state and national levels of government, rededicating themselves to the Founding notion that they (and any agencies they oversee) "derive their just powers from the consent of the governed," as opposed to serving as arbitrary, dictatorial entities. (1a, 1b)

Candidates who can successfully pass a post-graduate, college-level test on the contents of the U.S. Constitution (and one or more state constitutions, if applicable), the Bill of Rights, the Declaration of Independence, the Federalist Papers, and the old Articles of Confederation; individuals who can prove their fitness for public office by having pursued studies (self-taught or otherwise) that provide a factual, comparative analysis of various forms of governance — from "pure" democracies to socialist and communistic and totalitarian regimes. In that vein, candidates must also have a passing familiarity with the Declarations and Proclamations of the United Nations so as to be capable of intelligently dealing with that body. (1a, 1b, 3a)

Federal lawmakers must be subject to term limits of 8 years in the House and 12 years in the Senate, a timeframe which provides for needed experience, while ending the phenomenon known as the "career politician." (1a, 2a)

Salaries, "perks" and benefits of elected representatives and officials must be held to levels that represent a median compensation for comparable work in the private sector so as to avert elitism and help assure accountability. (1a, 2b)

No single agency of government can hold power greater than the people's elected representatives, and no elected representative can attest to powers greater than the legal citizenry that keeps him or her in office. Officials and department heads that practice or profess otherwise should be removed, and their agencies reconfigured, defunded or eliminated. The practice whereby politicians and bureaucrats begin their careers in government, then "leverage" their way into Washington's private sector, emerging as lobbyists and consultants as a means of retaining influence must be held to a set of strict guidelines to preclude the development of a proxy government. (1b)

A ban must be placed on the practice of tagging non-germane "earmarks" and "riders" onto legislation; as such action is an affront to the political process as conceived by the Framers. (1c)

Every federal program and expenditure must be subject to a five-year review, or else "sunsetted" in the event that no review is forthcoming (which indicates a lack of support for the program's continuance). (1c)

Any piece of legislation or practice which authorizes another nation or group of countries (e.g., the United Nations) to impose a tax, levy, fee or royalty upon the United States and its citizens, or which attempts to implement additional provisions to any non-ratified treaty, goes against constitutional intent and is, therefore, unsupportable. (1c, 3c, 3a)

If federal and the Internal Revenue Service can mail notices to nearly every household concerning completion of annual tax forms, then it has a duty to see that voting packets are mailed (or made easily available) to registered voters prior to election time; packets must contain required biographical data, a general statement as to the candidate's philosophy of government and his or her stand(s) on the issues facing state or local constituents in the candidate's district (national issues, if the position is for the U.S. Congress or President and Vice-President), plus a list of any local referendums with a generic "pro" and "con" side clearly set out, complete with any contact information or a website that might be helpful for additional information. (1d)

It is altogether fitting in a mobile, transient society that each State of the Union has its own unique constitution which affirms ideals contained in the U.S. Constitution, but which also retains enough independence from the federal entity to address issues important to their constituents so that individuals and businesses can more easily make decisions to relocate, as necessary, in keeping with their goals. (1d, 2b)

At no level — local, state or federal — does government have the right to define, license or restrict personal relationships, sexual or otherwise, *unless* there exists an issue involving matters of public health that poses demonstrable harm to other individuals. By the same token, the State has no right to dictate the standards of a *private* organization, such as a church or youth group, which are set for members who join of their own volition. (1e)

"Political correctness," originally a creation of totalitarian regimes, which went by various similar-sounding monikers under Adolf Hitler, Vladimir Lenin and Josef Stalin, inhibits any constitutional rights to free speech, assembly, belief and free conscience, usually beginning by twisting such ideals as "fairness."

Any entity seeking to coerce or manipulate private opinions via appeals to political correctness — be it an activist group, "resident assistants" (i.e., informants) in college dormitories, a union, a professional association or even an organization masquerading as a religious entity — must be exposed as illegitimate and de-funded where applicable. (1e, 4a)

Legislative and administrative procedures that infringe on the 4th Amendment, guaranteeing individual security and "a reasonable expectation of privacy" in one's person, property, papers or effects against unreasonable searches and seizures without a warrant (including the collection and storage of personal and family data), is intolerable, and legislation must be crafted to stem this threat to individual and national security. (1e, 5c, 4b)

Legislation or practice that permits takeovers of private property through "eminent domain" for any purpose other than actual, physical use by the government in the interests of national defense or public health compromises constitutional guarantees. If the intention is to provide benefit to all citizens, as in public parks and virgin wildernesses, a national referendum of such initiative must be sought prior to delegating any authority to invoke "eminent domain." Any foreign power, local township or nongovernmental organization (NGO) that attempts to invalidate individual prerogatives relating to rightfully owned property shall be penalized by the U.S. Dept. of Justice. (1f, 7b, 10a)

Protection of private property rights is a sacrosanct duty of government. The Nation's legal citizens, therefore, have the right to benefit from the fruits of their labors and free and unencumbered use of their own private and personal properties without underhanded special interests and governmental agencies compromising this important constitutional guarantee. The expansion of both governmental and non-governmental power (e.g., via environmental agencies and extremist groups) over private and personal property at the expense of the individual cannot be tolerated under the Constitution. (2b, 1f & 10a, 10b)

A culture of merit is impossible without a measure of personal risk, whereas an entitlement culture seeks to absolve the public of risk with utopian promises of security. Because the latter is incompatible with the Founders' vision of unfettered free enterprise under a "risk-and-reward" model, entitlement spending cannot be supported. (2c, 7c)

The concept of a "safety net" for individuals who overextend their finances or who, through no cause of their own making, suddenly find themselves without means, has its roots in compassion. Charitable organizations, including religiously based ones, should be freed of red tape, petty interference and over-regulation so that *they* may be empowered to more easily solicit private donations and in-kind aid for issues related to health, hunger, homelessness, debt, poverty, drug addiction and other causes that might otherwise not be supported by the electorate. (2b, 2c, 2d & 5c)

The Social Security and Medicare system, inaugurated following the Great Depression, is in financial trouble and cannot sustain itself on a permanent basis without vast increases in taxes on an already overburdened Generations X and Y. Therefore, it is in the interests of long-term economic policy to come up with a plan that would phase out the program in 40 years' time and encourage savings, while still providing for present retirees, including aging Boomers nearing retirement, all of whom were *forced* to pay a considerable portion of their income into both programs, so that they receive the full amount they are owed. Upon the demise of the Boomer generation, however, socialist-style programs like these should be made optional, and replaced with a risk-and-reward model as conceived by the Framers of the Constitution. (2b, 2d, 7f)

Lawmakers must return religious expression to its original legitimacy and cease dignifying frivolous lawsuits aimed at marginalizing and ridiculing traditions and principles that formerly were part and parcel of this nation's legal, ethical and moral heritage. (2e)

The U.S. Territories, which pay no taxes, should not be recipients of the same benefits and rights as the citizens of tax-paying states. (3b)

Inasmuch as English is the unifying language of the Nation, and as such impacts both national sovereignty and national security, no agency of government shall *mandate* the use of any other language for use within the continental United States. (3b, 4c, 11c)

The United Nations has been allowed to become seeded with leftist leaders in the mistaken belief that

American values and ideals will somehow "rub off" on backward and hostile nations. In light of the failure of that body to resolve or alleviate virtually any issue involving global security — from nuclear blackmail and proliferation via the International Atomic Energy Agency (IAEA) to world literacy the United Nations Educational, Scientific and Cultural Organization (UNESCO) to energy consumption — serious consideration must be given to defunding that ineffective body and re-allocating dollars already committed toward efforts that may prove more cost-effective. (3a, 4a)

No further foreign aid, humanitarian or otherwise, should be transferred from American taxpayers to hostile countries or their proxies; any such efforts deemed appropriate by citizens should be privately funded with the caveat that they carry an American flag and name of the donating organization(s), so that recipients can confirm where the aid came from. (3c, 4a, 7j)

Americans are not well-served by the trend, since the 1970s, of engaging in "police actions" — under whatever operational name — in which our Nation's military are deployed to foreign lands either to execute a limited, surgical strike or to "nation-build" (a term modeled on the Marshall Plan following World War II) but which has since resulted in protracted battles against well-armed, committed enemies. Any deployment of the Nation's troops must be preceded by a formal Declaration of War by Congress. This will go a long way toward diminishing what are presently seen as "quagmires" — never-ending operations without a clear objective; arguments over civilian casualties; and extended interment of enemy combatants. (3c, 6b)

A case must be brought before the U.S. Supreme Court to determine the interpretation and applicability of certain arcane language contained writings related to the original penning of the 14th Amendment, which gives citizenship to "all" children born in the U.S., but which apparently came with certain exclusions hinging on the term "ligiance" (an Old English word meaning "connection between sovereign and subject by which they were mutually bound, the former to protection and the *securing* of justice, the latter to *faithful service...*") and "subject to the jurisdiction thereof" (a clause effectively barring the offspring of foreign ministers, consuls, diplomats and other foreign subjects, excluding them from automatic U.S. birthright and serving as a qualifier to the term "all". Moreover, parents may *not* be subject to the jurisdiction of the U.S., *but rather to that of a foreign government.* This could be a game-changer in the illegal immigration debate.[14] (4c)

Local and state agencies of government have no business becoming entangled in frivolous lawsuits aimed at abridging the right of free speech, assembly and religious expression, such as Loudoun County, Virginia's recent effort to remove historic landmarks having Christian and Jewish icons that have existed for decades

---

[14] Source reference: Gerald Walpin, New York attorney and former inspector general for the Corporation for National and Community Service.

in full, public view. The trend of caving to every *pro bono* lawsuit initiated by opportunistic and politicized organizations (e.g., ACLU, ACORN) must be stopped where they begin — at the community, county and township levels. The courts must support this position, refusing to consider cases on appeal that step over this line. (4e)

For the first time, in the 21st century, the largest segment of unionized workers in America is comprised of government employees. The socialist-style movement that originally managed to get a foot in the door of American politics by promising to fight for better working conditions and wages has morphed into a force that now fights to *raise* their taxes even while threatening their livelihoods with a combination of inflammatory rhetoric, gratuitous strikes and unrealistic salary demands. A rabble-roused force of unionized government employees can easily be conscripted to intimidate the rest of the citizenry, much as Adolf Hitler's SS and Hitler's Youth intimidated and reported on "uncooperative" individuals and groups who did not agree with the Third Reich's policies. For all these reasons, unionization of government employees must be revoked, by constitutional amendment if necessary. (6c, 2b)

Government no longer has any place in regulating, arbitrating or maintaining agencies for matters relating to race, ethnicity or "diversity," as such efforts exacerbate rifts that are either disappearing or improving on their own. (5d)

The criminal justice system, together with law enforcement and the courts, comprises America's largest government agency. Trials take too long and cost too much. The system as a whole sustains a high recidivism rate and fails to protect the public that pays for it. Millions of dollars are spent on revenue enhancement and "*uber*-criminalization," both designed to intimidate and acclimate the populace to obeying petty restraints on their freedom. Therefore, the entire federal code, as well as the criminal justice system, must be overhauled so that "crime" encompasses only those offenses that are truly seditious and dangerous, and the courts and law enforcement perform only those functions the public properly expects. (5a-d)

War crimes, including jihadist attacks, committed by *foreign nationals* (a.k.a. *combatants, extremists, insurgents, militants*) must be addressed in a military court, leaving America's criminal justice system free to pursue criminal enterprises committed by home-grown offenders. (6a, 4b)

The current concept of "free trade," which is no longer a boon to the American worker, attempts to "buy" the good will and friendship of other countries by purchasing its goods *without the expectation of reciprocity*. Therefore, free trade must be reconfigured to look less like foreign aid and more like a business arrangement between entities of good will. (7a)

Wholesale federalization and nationalization of enterprises — including, but not limited to, student loans, automobile manufacturing, banking, health care, and mortgage lending — shall cease, as such action promotes irresponsibility and is inconsistent with a free-market economy. (7b)

Public-private partnerships and quasi-governmental institutions (among them Freddie Mac and Fannie Mae) blur the lines between private enterprise and tax-supported ventures, making federalization all the easier; therefore, the practice of government agencies encouraging partnership-style incentives must be discontinued permanently. (7d)

The tax code must be completely overhauled, as it has become overly time-consuming, burdensome, and expensively complicated not only for individual taxpayers, but for businesses, corporations and even government itself. In particular, personal and corporate tax rates must be reduced without shifting the tax burden from one income bracket to another, so that individuals and enterprises (**not** government!) will be encouraged to "grow the economic pie," create jobs and generate increased revenues over the long term. (7f)

The U.S. Treasury shall not print money as a solution to deficit spending, debt, and other government-caused financial woes, as this inflationary, currency-devaluing practice produces a vicious cycle of tax-and-spend from which no nation can expect to emerge unscathed. (7h)

All agencies, projects, and discretionary spending must be examined immediately, not only by economic experts, but by experienced individuals in *each of the affected fields*, with a view to rooting out waste, fraud, abuse, and frivolous investment. (7f)

Wage and price controls, by whatever name they are called (e.g., "rent control," "public housing") must be scuttled, as they foster a climate of dependency and sloth. However, private charities should be free to raise funds for whatever efforts they wish, the price tag resting on their own initiatives to raise money and secure backing from other private entities. (7g, 2d)

A newer, more welcoming environment for private enterprise, manufacturing and productivity must be created at home to stop the present massive outsourcing of jobs overseas. This necessarily entails re-thinking government regulation of the private sector and the self-employed (the FICA income limit alone may rise by some 15% of net for the self-employed in 2011), as well as minimum-wage laws and coercive unionization tactics.[15] (7e)

For catastrophic medical needs like birth defects and cancer, policies must be established that combine tax incentives with removal of red tape so that private charities, rather than government, are encouraged to construct free hospitals and locate doctors and staff who will do part-time *pro bono* work on behalf of the needy (in the model of the Scottish Rite and St. Jude Hospitals). (7j, 8b)

---

[15]   The National Education Association serves as a poster-child for coercive unionization tactics.

The present health-care debacle demands a multifaceted approach which, so far, has been made worse by government regulation and micromanagement. Simplistic "fixes," such as requiring every individual to purchase health insurance and every business to provide it, cannot begin to address the issues that are contributing to the Nation's current health care woes. The entire health-care challenge must be reconsidered with a view to encouraging the medical profession to correct systemic flaws brought on by a combination of new technologies, insurance scam-artists and counterproductive regulatory practices. A few examples (8a-c):

- o Drug-enforcement policies need to be overhauled so that those in pain get their medications without a hassle.

- o The medical profession also needs to see that Congress revamps privacy regulations that discourage family involvement (leading ultimately to a lack of critical patient information).

- o Federal and state funding should not be pressuring individuals to pursue expensive, exceedingly painful, experimental options with poor track records of success at the threat of being charged with medical negligence, or by the present practice of allocating grant monies based on the number of people who agree to certain procedures.

- Government should recognize that mandated health-insurance schemes, without the benefit of interstate competition, create a climate in which insurers cover little and charge a fortune in premiums, while hospital emergency rooms are awash in caring for the indigent and illegal aliens.

Medical ethics must be overhauled with a view to averting a looming culture of devalued life, among them (8a, 8c):

- easy acceptance of euthanasia;

- psychotropic drugging of children and "difficult" nursing home patients;

- nonconsensual human experimentation, including the use of misrepresented experimental drugs;

- harvesting and sale of organs, tissues (fetal and otherwise) and human eggs; surrogate pregnancies (and its accompanying legal horrors); and

- policy-making that discourages family involvement in medical decisions under a pretense of "privacy."

Tax-supported abortion, whether one is privately for or against it, is a Pandora's Box of medical ethics problems, leading to government-subsidized eugenics, population-control schemes (such as forced genetic counseling with accompanying politically correct parenting policies), and unsanctioned human experimentation. This must be addressed immediately. (8c)

Several issues surrounding the burgeoning and controversial mental health industry cry out for vigorous investigation by the U.S. Department of Justice. These are not being pursued because the Justice Department itself has a vested interest in many aspects of the various injustices being perpetrated. These include, but are not limited to (8c):

o involuntary collection and storage of personal information;

o data-sharing among agencies, especially since the 9/11 attacks;

o behavioral (not ethnic) profiling of anybody on the pretext that they may pose a threat; involuntary commitment of nonconformists to a mental-health facility;

o the push toward government-mandated mental health "parity" in health-insurance coverage; and

o the effort to "medicalize" behavior through labels of psychiatric "diseases" (as listed in the newest version of the *Diagnostic and Statistical Manual of Mental Disorders*, or DSM-V) for which there exist no definitive tests or standards, but have, by default, received the tacit approval of government.

American cities are awash in 1940s-era infrastructures, whether it is electrical power grids, roads and freeways, gas distribution systems, sewer lines or even communications links. Only in newer buildings and communities is there any kind of dependability without frequent power outages, massive gridlock, and equipment grown susceptible to damage due to neglect. Such large-scale infrastructure projects can no longer be dealt with as isolated incidents, with backup generators going mainly to government buildings and the extremely wealthy. Government must promote ambitious, permanent solutions; focused programs of research and development and, most of all, legislative action. *Fewer dollars must be spent providing infrastructure to hostile countries when our own cities need an extreme makeover.* (9a, 4a)

Thought must be given to utilizing knowledge already gained through the space program — the National Aeronautics and Space Administration (NASA) — to solve the Nation's energy needs; in particular, construction of geosynchronous orbiting solar collectors that microwave energy to large swaths of Earth-based receivers placed strategically in cloudless environments that otherwise are uninhabitable, such as the Mojave Desert. (9b, 10c)

Commitment to long-term energy independence must be augmented by (a) utilizing the vast reserves of fossil fuels here at home and (b) constructing reliable and safe nuclear power plants, under the direction of committed scientists. (9b, 10c)

Government agencies that misrepresent or disguise their mission, goals and operations must be either shut down or reorganized (e.g., the Environmental Protection Agency, which ostensibly works to identify harmful pollutants and protect animal and plant species but, in reality, advances counterproductive policies of wealth redistribution, limited property rights, "junk science" and crowded communities. (10a, 10b & 10c)

Government has a legitimate role to play in large-scale projects that do not lend themselves to privatization, such as augmenting of the nation's transportation needs, assuring energy independence, and replacing our 1940s-era infrastructure using equipment compatible with the quantum leaps in space-age technology, nuclear power and digitization. Agencies whose missions can be fulfilled by private entities, such as the National Endowment for the Humanities, should be defunded and eliminated to accommodate these kinds of ambitious projects. (11a)

The U.S. government must end its virtual monopoly over education policy. Private entities do a better job of raising literacy and assimilating newcomers. In phasing out the U.S. Department of Education, aligned governmental agencies (such as state education agencies) and quasi-governmental entities (e.g., the Council of Chief State School Officers, the Carnegie Foundation for the Advancement of Teaching) must lose their government subsidies. Government must also cut its ties to, and rescind tax breaks for, agenda-driven entities masquerading as professional organizations (e.g., the National Education Association, the Robert Wood Johnson Foundation, etc.). Red tape must be cut so that private entities might launch more private educational options, and even franchise them. With this approach (a) schooling will become more individualized; (b) education will be made less costly for parents; and (c) schools will become the smaller, nurturing, family-friendly entities they ought to be. (11a-11f, 7i)

Section 7.- **THIRD PARTIES: THEIR HISTORY, INFLUENCE AND POTENTIAL**

The Tea Party and Its Namesake

In April 2009, the "Tea Party" — an anti-tax, pro-constitutionalist, grassroots rally — launched a campaign that took its name from the Boston Tea Party, evoking images, slogans, and themes from a similarly fed-up-with-overbearing-government mindset that emerged in reaction to the British Parliament and Crown (King George III) on December 16, 1773. At the time, Britain had adopted last-straw policies aimed at colonists to help pay costs ostensibly associated with keeping them in the Empire. The British government imposed a series of direct taxes — the Stamp Act, followed by still other laws (dubbed "Intolerable Acts" by colonial leaders) that were intended, at least in part, as a demonstration of British authority. There are parallels today in the United States. Much of the overregulation we see today, which far exceeds that of just 30 years ago, has a partial objective of reminding U.S. citizens just who is in charge. This has the subtle effect of reducing "We the People" to underlings, or subjects. The Founding documents took the position that the government worked for the people, not that the people were the government's subjects, or wards. The result of the latter perception is that an ideology that allows government "experts" to remake the society and culture into a model altogether different from what the Framers intended.

When a tea tax was imposed as a demonstration of British power, it was aimed at generating revenue. But it was also a taunt, aimed at seeing just how much "authority" Britain could get away with without incurring significant consequences. One can see parallels today in the U.S., as outrageous pieces of legislation like "Cap-and-Trade," annual vehicle emissions checks, and even exorbitant fines of $500 for violating (even accidentally) dog leash laws all serve as a barometer of what the public will put up with.

As for Britain in 1773, Parliament soon had its answer: A group led by Samuel Adams, dressed to evoke American Indians, boarded the ships of the government-favored British East India Company and dumped the estimated £10,000 worth of tea on board into the Boston harbor to protest The Tea Act, which was, essentially, another burden upon the American colonists who had, by that time, little or no representation (or "say") as to how they were governed. New York and Philadelphia sent British ships, with its tea on board, back to Britain. In Charleston, the colonists left the tea on the docks to rot.

Reaction in Britain was swift. The tea tax was followed with more punitive shows of coercion: the Coercive Acts (the Massachusetts Government Act, altering the Massachusetts charter and restricting town meetings; the Administration of Justice Act, ordering all British soldiers suspected of crimes to be arraigned in Britain instead of in the colonies; the Boston Port Act, closing the port of Boston until such time as the British had been compensated for the tea lost in the Boston Tea Party fiasco; and the Quartering Act of 1774, allowing royal governors to house British troops in the homes of citizens without requiring permission of the owner.

All these were passed by the British Parliament to harass the colonists (and also generate revenue, of course). But these measures reminded the colonists that they still, technically, were citizens of the Empire. Together with other abuses, colonists became united in their frustration and inspired a revolt against their British masters — which, in turn, led to the American Revolution.

Sound familiar?

Today's taxpayers can relate. A large swath of Americans, until recently a loosely connected affiliation of constitutionally minded patriots in localities far removed from Washington, see themselves as similarly taunted and aggrieved by a self-aggrandizing, bloated government that is morphing into a collectivist super-State.

Even though recent pariahs, such as the Enron executives (who defrauded hundreds of shareholders out of their life's savings), Eliot Spitzer (disgraced former governor of New York) and Thomas E. Donilon (registered lobbyist from 1999-2005 for Fannie Mae, which suffered a massive accounting scandal during his tenure) seemed to receive their just deserts in the short term, most individuals of that caliber and wealth still manage to receive enormous severance packages, prorated bonuses, their own TV talk shows (e.g., Spitzer, with CNN) and even appointments to prestigious positions (e.g., National Security Advisor for Donilon) once the brouhaha has died down. Their influence helps sustain the government bureaucracy and keep certain statutes that work against the little guy in place.

Those of lesser means (a mere million dollars or so) who run afoul of the press and the authorities, however, are pilloried, usually permanently. This is what is meant by a "ruling elite" or an "elite caste system," something the Framers of our Constitution were anxious to prevent in America.

Added to overregulation, over-taxation and just plain overbearing government in general, modern-day citizens have been prompted into launch a new patriotic movement, which they dubbed the Tea Party. Its adherents posted a mission statement and a set of core principles online[16], portions of which readers of this document will find partially re-iterated and expanded upon in Section 5 of this booklet.

Today's Tea Party mirrors in some ways the 1773 revolutionaries who called themselves "Patriots," "Whigs," "Congressmen," or just plain "Americans." Together, they represented a full range of socio-economic classes and demographic groups united in their recognition of the need to defend individual rights.

The impetus for the Tea Party movement, in 1774 as now, boils down to excessive government: heavy and punitive taxes; harassment; and ever-expanding, oppressive regulations. While its advocates today do not

---

[16] The Tea Party mission statement and core principles can be found at http://teapartypatriots.org/Mission.aspx.

yet endorse outright rebellion, recent events (as described in Sections 1 and 2) have given even the wildest of the Boomer generation pause. The new Tea Party wants to attract, educate, organize, and mobilize citizens to reject the coming super-State and return policy making to the Framers' core values of Fiscal Responsibility, Constitutionally Limited Government and Free Markets before the "other shoe" drops.

Unfortunately, today's Tea Party movement is experiencing what many third party efforts before it contended with — aggressive attempts by provocateurs and hangers-on to water down or infiltrate the movement, many of them either rejecting its goals or agreeing with some, but not others. Either way, the end result tends to be the same: gradual weakening and corruption of the new movement, with opportunists and special interests working to usurp control.

Which, of course, leaves the status quo securely in place.

The Middle Classes Ward Off Brickbats

Because consensus is king and a warped view of "fairness" essentially dominates the media, it is easy to divide and conquer new movements and marginalize their adherents, typically utilizing the tried-and-true allegations of racism, bigotry and intolerance. Typical examples include a flap over the leader of Montana's Big Sky Tea Party in September 2010, which involved a conversation on Facebook that the media claimed *could be interpreted* as condoning violence against homosexuals. The "interpretation" charge was a stretch, but it managed to send members running for cover and sparked resignations.

Another component, the Tea Party Express (an outgrowth of a political action committee, or PAC, in California), was expelled in July 2010 from the National Tea Party Federation when a key member, who happened to be a radio talk show host, was *accused* of writing a "racist" blog.

On and on it goes, a never-ending stream of allegations, fanciful interpretations and insinuations aimed at discrediting, piecemeal, every startup movement that is deemed a potential threat to the two most established political parties. Add to that an enormous government bureaucracy whose employees expect to remain in their jobs and get pensions upon retirement, and scores of foundations, institutes and non-governmental organizations which "partner" with government agencies, and you have a mighty force against the establishment of any third party that might "rock the boat."

Thus has the objective of restoring the Founders' vision of a Republic become a tug-of-war for support between disorganized factions, each clamoring for its own objectives, but through the lens of constitutional government. If the group in question is not well organized or is funded only in fits and starts, it will wither.

On the positive side, there are signs that Americans are tiring of same old tactics and excuses. For example, the "race-and-bigot card" is wearing thin, as is hostility to established religious groups — Catholics, Protestants, Mormons and Jews. They are tired of wars in which our government does not demand surrender. They are weary of deficits, fiscal mismanagement and tax money going to pay for things they would never have approved had they been asked.

The same goes for the barrage of unnecessary rules and nuisance regulations aimed directly at the backbone of society: the middle class. We may be a math-challenged nation, but most adults know that money, even adjusted for inflation, no longer buys what it did in their parents' day. They know that $250,000 a year isn't "rich," and that such an income will not send their offspring to private school or college, will not allow for a little beach bungalow somewhere on the shore, and will not replace appliances that now come with expensive motherboards and other electronics — all things middle-class folks once were able to afford. Yet, every time they turn on their televisions, they learn that their "betters" in Congress and disgraced CEOs are getting perks, bailouts and large severance packages — people who have rarely, if ever, stood in a grocery line, cut coupons or picked up their own cleaning.

Once the middle class has had enough, Big Government will either be in jeopardy — or it will have already amassed enough clout to tolerate no interference. Tea Partiers worry that the latter scenario is the likelier one, and they hope to head it off in time.

Successes and Failures of Third Party Candidates

Third party efforts have not fared especially well, primarily due to lack of organization, strategic skill, media savvy and, of course, funding. Wikipedia describes a multitude of third parties throughout the nineteenth century: the Prohibition Party, Greenback Party and the Populist Party, the latter evolving "from widespread antiparty sentiment and a belief that governance should attend to the public good rather than partisan agendas." Because their various positions "were based more on social experiences than any political ideology, nonpartisan activity was generally most effective on the local level."

There have probably been more parties than most people even know about: the Independence Party, the Independent Party (a.k.a. *America's Independent Party*), the Constitution Party, the Natural Law Party, the Green Party and more...

In politics, an **independent** or **non-party** politician usually means an individual not affiliated with any established political party. Independents may hold centrist positions between any of the major political parties, or they may have a viewpoint based on issues they do not feel any major party addresses. Still other independent candidates *are* associated with a major political party and may even be former members, but choose not to stand under its label as a candidate. A third category of independents are those who may belong to or support a political party, but believe they should not formally represent it and thus be subject to its policies.

Finally, some independent candidates may form their own political party for the purpose of running for public office. John B. Anderson ran as an Independent in 1980 with something under 6 million votes and, as is typical, zero electoral votes.

H. Ross Perot was a natural beneficiary of populist resentment toward establishment politicians, with his folksy style and "plainspeak" charts and graphs — not to mention a successful track record in business. In May 1992, he was featured on the cover of *Time Magazine* with the title "Waiting for Perot," an allusion to Samuel Beckett's famous play. In the 1992 election, he received 18.9 percent of the popular vote, (but again, no electoral votes), making him the most successful third-party presidential candidate in terms of the popular vote since Theodore Roosevelt in the 1912. With that, the vested political interests took note and thought "oh-oh."

A tiny few third party candidates *have* won electoral votes: Strom Thurmond had 39 in 1948, George Wallace got 46 in 1968 and John Hospers managed just one in 1972. Compared with Thurmond and Wallace, who polled very strongly in a small number of states, Perot's vote was more evenly spread across the country. In 1995, Perot founded the Reform Party and won its nomination for the 1996 election. But because of ballot-access laws, he still had to run as an Independent in many states. Perot received eight percent of the popular vote in 1996, much less than he did in the 1992 race, but still an unusually successful third-party showing by U.S. standards. But he spent much less of his own money in this race than he had four years before, and also allowed other people to contribute to his campaign, unlike in his prior race.

A common explanation for Perot's failure to do better was his exclusion from the presidential debates, something the media controls in conjunction with the preferences of the Democratic and Republican parties (described more fully by George Farah in his book, *Open Debates*).

Cozy Relationships: Key to Success with Media

Between 1992 and 1996, the Commission on Presidential Debates had changed its rules regarding qualification procedures for candidates in the presidential debates. Perot had previously done very well in debates owing to his gift of simplifying complex ideas for average Americans, so it was a blow to his, and other, campaigns when the Commission ruled that he could not participate, as he had not yet been endorsed by "a substantial number of major news organizations" — the term *substantial* and *news organizations* being the operative terms. The mainstream press viewed Perot as a charismatic threat. Ronald Reagan had taught the press a thing or two about underestimating charismatic people. Accustomed since Watergate to wielding authority, the press liked neither Pat Buchanan nor Ross Perot in 1992 and 1996; nor Ron Paul in 1988 and

2008; nor "Dubya" in 2004 and 2008. So they worked to neutralize their candidacies.

But news pundits and journalists were soon in for a shock, as the Internet, coupled with vastly expanded digital band-widths, began leveling the *media's* playing field. Even search engine giants could not effectively control the Internet beast. Suddenly the Big Three networks weren't the only games in town, nor were the old-standby print newspapers, magazines and periodical publications. The only "ace-in-the-hole" was a global network of accumulated wealth, not all of it from average investors. Intimidation and kickbacks, for example, were easy methods of neutralizing the opposition. Some political factions, therefore, would suddenly surprise everyone by actually welcoming (or at least including) previously abhorred groups — pro-lifers, "flat-taxers" and gay-lobby groups, environmentalist activists — as situations dictated. The strategy of courting the opposition proved highly successful for ethically challenged entities at both ends of the political spectrum, because doing so leads ultimately to a successful gambit to "divide-and-conquer" the competition.

This should have been a wake-up call to constitutional purists, when an individual candidate can be censored or legitimized, in effect, by the two major political parties with the help of the media. It is an indication that the two-party system (and therefore government itself) is up to its ears in corruption.

Smaller factions, analogous to 2009's Tea Party

movement have, since the 1960s, cropped up here and there. Take, for example, Howard Arnold Jarvis (September 22, 1903 – August 11, 1986), a businessman, lobbyist, and politician-turned-anti-tax activist. He coined the slogan "Mad As Hell and Not Going to Take It Anymore," and was responsible for a massive property tax-cutting initiative (California's Proposition 13, passed in 1978), as well as a mini-tax revolt. Ironically, the revolt ended up launching rent control, with some landlords pocketing their property-tax savings. With that, Jarvis' movement died with cries of "I told you so" from committed collectivists, but his idea and slogan remained in the public mind.

Third-Party Influence Brokers

Third-party candidates have tried, without much lasting success, to insert themselves into mainstream politics. They became caught up in party-like foundations, associations and interest groups and wound up aligning with partisan leaders to fund their operations. The alliances and the factions they brought in discouraged many nonpartisan supporters and undermined their capability to form a large support base. Worse, most third parties were never able to produce a coherent, rational platform, so they had no basis from which to work, save for a few pet peeves.

Many reformers and nonpartisans subsequently returned to what by then were seen as "legitimate" political parties — the Republican Party and Democrat

Party — which occasionally promised to reverse their stand on issues important to key interest groups — slavery (eventually recast as "civil rights") or prohibition (eventually revitalized as "substance abuse"). But that lasted only so long as the issues in question had something they wanted. For example, the race card can be played in all sorts of ways that have nothing to do with discrimination; substance abuse can be used as an excuse to raise taxes (for rehabilitation, psychiatric services and the "War on Drugs") as well as to electronically track individual prescription purchases.

Not all third party movements, of course, have been either "conservative" or "liberal," "traditionalist" or "libertarian." For example, two separate Progressive Parties, the Green Party, the Socialist Party, even the Communist Party USA. A recent such faction actually calls itself the Third Party Movement[17] — more a quasi-peace-and-love, anarchistic group than any sort of patriotic resurgence.

Further confusing the liberal- conservative archetypes are the Natural Law Party (founded in 1992, based on the ideas of Maharishi Mahesh Yogi and the Transcendental Meditation movement), and two different Progressive Parties, one created by a split in the Republican Party during the presidential election of 1912, and the other, the Progressive Democrats of America, founded during the 2004 Democratic National Convention in Massachusetts. The latter helped launch the presidential campaigns of Howard Dean and Dennis Kucinich.

---

[17]   http://thethirdpartymovement.com/

Most people equated term *progressive* with *socialism* long before 2004, however, mainly because of John Dewey's highly publicized "progressive education" of the 1920s and 30s. He denounced, in effect, all academics in favor of socializing a child below college age. That he went on to promote atheism and, later, Marxism prompted many to associate all four together — progressivism, atheism, Marxism and socialism — despite the factual particulars, which goes to show the power of the media.

Thus, the "progressive" label, while connoting modernization, carried baggage for American political reformers who wanted to shed the Marxist-socialist label. But the term was very convenient for educators who slid through UNESCO's back door right into U.S. classrooms. Moreover, the Progressive Party of the Dewey era produced a sea-change in America's perceptions about government even if it didn't win its candidates a single congressional or presidential seat — not officially, anyway.

While the Reform Party USA starring Ross Perot was expected to break the cycle of third party failures at the polls, that didn't happen. Perot was (and remains) a billionaire Texas businessman with a gift for presenting complex fiscal and other policy concepts via charts and graphs. But his political ambitions proved to be short-lived once he experienced first-hand the intimidation of today's political environment. When a like-minded former wrestling champion named Jesse Ventura took the mantra of the Reform Party in 1997, however, he became governor of Minnesota, and people expected the

Party to rebound. But the Reform Party never really "jelled," for all the usual reasons related to lack of a comprehensive strategy, a well-defined platform, organizational know-how and public relations.

More accepted has been the Libertarian Party, which has enjoyed some limited success since its founding in 1971 to "challenge the cult of the omnipotent state and defend the rights of the individual." It is host to the well-endowed libertarian think-tank, the Cato Institute, Washington, D.C., established in 1977.

Libertarianism eschews the labels of both "liberal" and "conservative," preferring to align itself more toward a Jeffersonian philosophy that focuses more on fiscal issues than social ones and preferring the term "market liberalism" as a categorical descriptor. Libertarianism does favor individualism over conformity and collectivism, which of course moves into the social-issue realm, and so it gained adherents from the likes of Rep. Ron Paul and his son, Rand. Ron attempted to run for President in 2008 but, like Perot and Pat Buchanan, he found himself outmaneuvered by a hostile press, which ignored their large constituencies.

The View Ahead for Third Parties

Patriotic conservatives without political sophistication remain baffled as to why they do not seem to be making headway, especially in local elections. What they don't see is the often sudden infusion of funds to candidates from well-endowed organizations whenever it is perceived that a new kind of candidate might win. This problem has moved today's Tea Party activists to work toward a different paradigm, one in which prospective candidates sign on to Tea Party ideals so as to garner its leaders' endorsement, as opposed to establishing a political party outright and then funding official candidates for elections.

Determined to avoid the pitfalls of previous attempts at Third Party activism and facing a burgeoning Nanny State, modern-day "Tea-Partiers" (as they call themselves) are working on their media skills ("you betcha, Sarah Palin") and computer savvy so as to be able to nail the opposition whenever it tries to sell a bait-and-switch routine to the public.

Initially, Tea-Partiers retooled the TEA acronym into the slogan "Taxed Enough Already." But even wholehearted advocates soon recognized that taxes were only the tip of the iceberg that characterizes the creeping heavy-handedness of government in domestic, social, fiscal and foreign policy. More than that, though, it has become impossible to ignore the interconnected, wide range of overreaches that increasingly shuts out average citizens under the pretense of empowering them — the much-touted, but fully choreographed, town-hall-style meeting being but one example.

Which leaves the fate of the Tea Party in limbo despite some wins in the primaries.

Obviously, much has changed in American society since the days of the Revolutionary War and the ratification of the U.S. Constitution, especially with respect to the huge leaps of technology and scientific achievement. Ethics, however, have not kept up with technological progress, and the courts remain behind the curve of events instead of ahead of them. This situation has had the unfortunate side-effect of eroding constitutional principles, values and ideals in a modern world that is sinking under the weight of high-tech gadgets. Movements like the Tea Party are discovering there is no "*app* for that."

Which leads us to reconsider the Revolutionary-era patriot whose great tome published in 1776, *Common Sense*, is today mostly censored from modern classrooms. Dedicated to the primacy of reason, Thomas Paine (like Ross Perot some 200 years later) distilled complex ideas and made them intelligible to average readers of his day, using a clear, concise writing style that appealed both to the average, even marginally educated, person at the time. Yet, Paine also managed to resonate with the more formal, learned lots that were among his contemporaries. Whether a third party can accomplish that today remains to be seen.

Even so, it is in the vein of Thomas Paine's political writings and his vision of a democratic republic that a Rational, Common Sense Platform is constructed. The country needs leaders (and thus candidates) who represent and articulate convictions and principles, individuals unafraid to announce a reversal of opinion based upon a "maturing of thought" over time, also known as a "re-assessment of the facts." The scripted, sound-bite mentality is, after all, no substitute for clear-headed deliberation.

The nation requires educated individuals having firm sets of well-considered beliefs and values. This is, of course, the antithesis of 1960s and 70s wisdom, first set forth in Benjamin Bloom's *Taxonomy for Educational Objectives* in 1978. Bloom insisted that the school's primary job was to "challenge a student's fixed beliefs."

That turned out to be an awful mistake in terms of educating the young. The goal of life is not to be so "flexible" that one changes convictions with the wind. Rather, the objective should be to *solidify* one's convictions based on study, experience and, above all, reason.

CONCLUSION

In summary, *A Common Sense Platform for the 21ˢᵗ Century* represents a starting point for true patriots committed to the ideals and principles of the Framers of the U.S. Constitution and the Bill of Rights, based on the Declaration of Independence. The Platform recognizes the genius of the Founders in anticipating progress, to the extent that they included a means for amending the American Constitution while keeping the original ideals and precepts intact.

Inasmuch as the major American political parties have declined to pursue the grave problems that threaten the life-blood of the Republic, a Common Sense approach, in the mode of Thomas Paine's great tome, can offer a viable strategy that combats both world government and returns us to a sovereign nation.

Moreover, it is the corrupt, two-party system that has outlived its usefulness, not the United States Constitution or its ideals. As it stands, however, any competing third parties, however worthy, remain too haphazard, fractionalized and ill-led to be successful.

For all these reasons the Common Sense Platform is constructed so that its tone harkens back to that remarkable (and refreshing) period when issues were deliberated logically, but forcefully; when basic principles and tenets could be cited without appearing trite; when people conducted themselves with some degree of propriety, but minus the lockstep "conformity." Thus do we owe a debt of gratitude to Thomas Paine and his 1776 booklet, *Common Sense*, which greatly influenced the Framers and hopefully will serve to revolutionize modern governance, now in peril, within these United States.

In accordance with the wishes of those who have expressed an interest in officially signing on to the above Common Sense Platform, and who, by confirming for themselves the accuracy of the various rationales (historical and legal) provided in this booklet as a context for this Platform, the following attestation is presented below for your convenience.

ATTESTATION

I, the undersigned candidate for the office of _____, do maintain and affirm that government serves at the pleasure of, and belongs exclusively to, its legal citizenry. In attestation of this fact, I hereby affirm that I subscribe to and will advocate for at least **85 percent** of the precepts, resolutions and principles articulated in this document, and will provide reasons why I do not agree with the others. I pledge that I will bear true and steadfast allegiance to the legal electorate I represent by actively and demonstrably initiating, promoting and supporting legislation and practice in the furtherance of same. I further solemnly proclaim that I will faithfully discharge the duties of the office I hold in the best interests of my *constituents* and the *legal* citizenry of the United States of America, and will, to the utmost of my ability, act to preserve, protect, support and defend the Constitution of the State I represent, as well as the Constitution of the United States of America, against all enemies, foreign or domestic. So I do swear upon my honor and my word.

_____

Candidate

_____

Prospective Office

_____

Witness

_____

Notary

About B. K. Eakman

As an educator, writer and researcher, Beverly Eakman is a veteran of 700 nationwide radio/TV talk shows and 200 speaking engagements with numerous published articles on education, mental health and privacy issues in national magazines.

Her columns and lectures have appeared in *Education Week*, *Chronicles Magazine*, *The Washington Times*, *Insight Magazine*, *National Review*, *Crisis Magazine*, *Vital Speeches*, *The Washington Post*, and more.

Her books, *Cloning of the American Mind: Eradicating Morality Through Education*, *Educating for the New World Order* and its sequel *Microchipped: How the Education Establishment Took Us Beyond Big Brother*, have been hailed as 'must reads' by parents, educators, medical doctors and reviewers.

Her latest book, *Walking Targets, How Our Psychologized Classrooms are Producing a Nation of Sitting Ducks*, exposes how our educational system is driving a wedge between parents and children, and acclimating the next generation to be both the wards and the targets of a Nanny State.

Midnight Whistler Publishers
http://www.midnightwhistler.com

www.ingramcontent.com/pod-product-compliance
Lightning Source LLC
Chambersburg PA
CBHW051430280526
45785CB00003B/1231